VICTIM OF DREAMS

CIVIL WAR IN THE SOUL

Jeremy Gluck

Jeremy Gluck

All rights reserved, no part of this publication may be reproduced by any means, electronic, mechanical photocopying, documentary, film or in any other format without prior written permission of the publisher.

>   Published by
>   Chipmunkapublishing
>   PO Box 6872
>   Brentwood
>   Essex CM13 1ZT
>   United Kingdom

http://www.chipmunkapublishing.com

Copyright © Jeremy Gluck 2009

Edited by Kayla Pratt

Cover Photography: Tyron Francis

Chipmunkapublishing gratefully acknowledge the support of Arts Council England.

Victim Of Dreams

Victim of Dreams

The closer reality draws
Dreams draw closer still
From metal to the grinder
The sparks fly
Cold and hard the realisation
While small lights swing and die
I have seen my brother in his asylum
His blood also mine

I have seen the future
And its number is one
I have seen my father in his dying
And am still his son

Demanding answers from God
I am handed His design
I will be alone
No rescue will find me
Salvation is a fiction
Redemption never was
What is real remains so
What is not fiery dust.

- Jeremy Gluck October 2006

Jeremy Gluck

Victim Of Dreams

Foreword

"Where Tao is, equilibrium is. When Tao is lost, out come all the differences of things."

- Tao Te Ching No. 18

This book was written intensively over six months between late 2006 and early 2007, and then in shorter bursts through the remainder of that year. I did not intend to write a book, merely to expand a loose memoir started years before to break in my first word processor. The Afterword talks more about the genesis of "Victim of Dreams"; here I want to introduce the manner of its construction. Italics are employed generally to signify material I brought from journals, letters and other archived sources; this material is edited little, if at all, in order to present the mental processes of my slippage. This is not, however, always the case, and the progress of the narrative will slip in its flow according to my intuition at time of writing. With this book I've tried to infer to the reader an inner world and reality, therefore external detail is wanting. I didn't plan this approach but it became the most authentic and interesting; its style is influenced by Burroughs, whose genius was to try to write his way *out* of life, whereas my attempt might be to write my way *in*. I have not canceled time and life with itself in order to suggest progress, preferring to leave events and experiences, reflections and realisations chaotic and raw. It would be easy but misleading to revise my words of memory, madness and insight to suit a new, "recovery" script that in the time since I completed the original manuscript has evolved out of the experiences it latterly describes.

This is the work of another book which I am yet to write. I do in the Afterword discuss my burgeoning recovery but the validity of my experience can only reside in its obstinate otherness and I've presented it as plainly as I can. It happened, just as did the events described, without any real architecture. The order, beauty and ambiguity of childhood soon gives way to the incipient chaos of bipolar onset. Pieces of my life have been omitted, truncated or skirted. What remains is the illness, its presentation and manifestation, in the life of one sufferer. Thoughts without captions. As I say in the manuscript, I don't want or expect to be understood...but felt, perhaps.

Jeremy and friend, about 1961, Sydney, Nova Scotia

Victim Of Dreams

Prologue: *"...out come all the differences of things."*

Earlier, before his first marriage and the war, my father had great success with his downtown hat store. Then, inexplicably, moving it to a less promising location where it foundered, he set the pattern I would follow years later and snatched defeat from the jaws of victory. My own success came early, too, and in volume. My dreams were nearly realised when, inexplicably, too, I circumvented their fulfilment. Stop-start the success tailed off in total and then the days of the desert began when, as my children were becoming more and more beautiful, my marriage flourished and then foundered,. The illness had begun before any of that, in rooms of strangeness I understood as spiritual struggle or loser's luck. Fell down I went on, in and out of myself, trying not to sink but finding the underwater world breathable and real. Walking became slow, but foreshortened vision – if not visions – permitted pain relief to the heart. The path became the ditch became the standstill hole my head revolved in for the sake of incoming insanity. My civil war began, battling with both my mind and another, elusive thinker, whose view of both of me had a unifying power: in its grip I was no more at war, but lost to peace. None of me made any sense and I waited out the winter in wonder, terror and sometimes ecstasy. But most of all I didn't wait out as much as want out, and it was that trajectory that one morning brought the standstill to its limits; I had to move, even to oblivion. The civil war in my soul had reached its natural climax: one casualty.

Hounded in the moment to extreme guilt, my psyche buckled. There were many causes, most of them the ragtag attrition of my selves. And there were other, silent reasons. The two people who damned me also saved me. I ended up in the local bin awaiting assessment. I warned the shrinks how articulate I am and not to trust my lucidity. Naturally, they decided to send me home. The wife cried and they decided to commit me. The wife saw the ward and cried differently and I went home.

After my psychotic episode I filled in a bipolar self-assessment I found online. I got the first perfect test score of my life. In the spring of 2002 I was diagnosed with bipolar disorder. I was forty-four. After diagnosis life began over again. Parts seemed unbearably wasted, like my marriage. Other parts became – gradually, as I was medicated and stabilised - somehow mythological to me, times and places where the one I was, before my new stranger, had held sway without opposition. I was still just as sick, one day answering to the concerned question of my still wife, How are you? with I'm dead. But it was not the same thing any more. I knew myself from scratch. I was being reborn without any idea how to grow up healthy. My love-hate relationship with myself was reduced to like-help. I still became crazy, but the conviction was waning. The jailhouse door stood ajar.

Victim Of Dreams

My First Life

I was sitting in my parents' kitchen. Maybe it was 1971. Paper popped out of my three-ring binder was piled on the table. On the top page I'd written some disjointed but themed lines, beginning, *Life is just one meaningless event after another*. Others said more or less the same thing, and I read them again and again as they were written. My father came upstairs; for once he wasn't working late. He paused by me, skimmed my lines and smiled to himself, or at least to a part of himself. I think he asked me if I meant it. He was proud of me: few things in a twelve year old can be more precocious than despair.

I remember every detail of that kitchen, the chipped round slots in the storm window frames I swung up a ladder every October. The tall broom cupboard? I can see its door, but nothing inside it. I can see my life from the front, and nothing inside it, too. Memory is not unreliable or deceptive, it's random. The average is nothing if not detailed. For example, the Sixties silver toaster, its shape and elements, its brittle black plastic and now primitive handle. I can see that but not any detail of my mother's face of the time, not that isn't copped and cropped from a long-lost photograph and clipped to something somewhere else in my memory. Now that Mom is dead I don't feel any need to remember her with clarity, but it does seem strange that I can't. We can intimate from how we forget our parents how others will forget us. We can't "remember" people dead, which is a shame, because that's the one time most might make a lasting impression.

The fan over the stove was that very dull yellow you get with enamel made greasy. It matched the fridge. I think the floor was black. I can look out the kitchen window to the lawn, in winter, when it didn't condemn us with its neglect.

1936 My father and his siblings, he stands 2nd from right

Victim Of Dreams

In those days the classrooms seemed to have genuine differences but come back to me as walls of drawers with scale toys rattling around them, names and faces with no independent power. The place was like the *Poseidon* upright, but adrift and listing. Straight but slanted. I must have had a bad day at school, who knows what, and so I was in the kitchen churning out life-signs of the self-pity that would one day dictate many of my feelings and actions. I felt that nobody understood me, and I was as right as you get, but without the complementary, central realisation that nobody cares. The light in that kitchen created a begrudging introverted murkiness that, when we ate together and my older brother wasn't there to bend the mood, and Dad was home and making faces so funny I gagged my food down between howls, could be radiant. What we feel moves our light around us. We feel and the light moves at it one way or another, not in a way science understands, but in way that accords with what certainty we're permitted.

That's just the kitchen, and it's as bright as daylight. There were more rooms, seen and felt by me now as they must have looked on the realtor's drawings, with their individual and then collective glow blue-inked, plain but with promise. And how one joined or connected or led to another; never underestimate the significance of how the rooms in one house join one another. Walking in and out of their light, down the always darker hallways, you feel the rooms in a very special way. The living room was full of light. The view across the street to Carol Anne's split-level was okay. It was a small, beautiful house, and I discovered plenty there.

The chief feature of the rec room was the train table. The people who owned the house before us, Reed or Reid, had two kids, one of each. John, the son, later went blind. The father had put a foldaway table in the wall big enough to take a serious HO layout; I saw it before we moved in, the time we viewed the house and John was at his Dad's workbench (where I would polish my father's shoes) showing me with pride his new novelty model dragster. That train set comes back to me forty years later, not an actual mental image of it, but an impression of something that even now lies beyond my experience, much less expertise. A symbol of a relationship to my father and myself, and within myself, and between my eyes and hands that I never have enjoyed. It is an "other kids" symbol, one more fleeting, present forever imprint of a thing others kids did or had that I didn't do or have, and soon enough didn't want, because they did things with their hands that were beautiful and mighty but their minds remained sterile. That's why even at ten I would steal away from the Atwells pleading a nap knowing they knew I was just bored with them and the predictability they perfected so young, the same steps they would take carrying their parcel through time, the one they'd never drop...or open. Even at ten I felt sorry for them, the way their parents must have felt sorry for skinny me. They looked at their kids and saw doctors and lawyers and teachers. So did my parents, but the difference was that my parents knew they were seeing a dumb mirage. My brother and I would

Victim Of Dreams

never be a doctor or a lawyer. We'd get sick and break the law. Come to think of it, I don't know what my parents saw. My mother saw me as a writer, which I always was, but she saw more than anything the writer she had always wanted to finish being. In a way that was her curse: not to finish being. That's the way it seems to me, but kids know about as much about their folks as their folks know about them.

There was a cookie jar like a big ripe apple. The toaster was under the cupboard by the window, then the stove, then the back door, the stairs to the basement, the fridge, the broom cupboard, then the kitchen door, then the cookie jar. The top cupboards held matzo meal and oats; my mother waged war on the ants hiding in them. Ben gave us a big freezer, but that was downstairs. Across the hallway the living room, my father's stereo – Dual turntable, AR speakers, a furry record cleaner (Dual) – and the hundreds of classical albums in alphabetical order. Dining table, four chairs, sideboard. A big couch and two chairs, with orange throws. A wide front window. Tall old lamp. On the trolley there was the samovar, a silver relic I think from Mom's side of the family, an incredible thing, ornate and unlikely. Up the hall three bedrooms, and a linen cupboard. My father never had a carport built (not enough room for a garage) so my brother and I were stuck digging the car out winter after winter. Before dawn, mid-December, she'd be outside your bedroom door and before you knew it you were shovel in hand, a scarf in your mouth, squinting.

Jeremy Gluck

My father picked his teeth at the table; it drove my mother nuts. She'd say, "Noel!" and then dissolve in laughter at his ludicrous grimaces and gesticulations. She called him "his Nibs". He liked spring onions in salt and pepper, and ate all the stuff I couldn't bring myself to: *borscht*, tongue, kidneys and liver. My love was *matzoh* balls, rubbery solids floated in chicken soup; the more I could get of them the better. I can't remember if Mom made *hamantaschen* - triangular poppy-seed Purim treats – or bought them from the mighty Rideau Bakery that, since the turn of the last century, and stubbornly using its original machinery, was a legend for its perfect output. Every week, along with thousands of others, including many converted *goyim,* my folks would make the pilgrimage there, returning with bags of rye bread, salt sticks and onion buns, the latter the subject of cult-like devotion and which they would later lay in for me before my annual visits. I wouldn't be an hour off the plane before I'd be polishing off three or four onion buns. In my teens it was Riverside Pizzeria that became the focus of food obsession, but the Rideau never lost its edge, and its antiquated diner counter and cases and colours whispered a time when was life simpler and tasted better.

My mother got a big kick out of a novelty cushion her kid sister Jean got her, with "Screw the Golden Years!" embroidered on it. I don't have much about what she wore. When she was young her furrier father made her and her sisters beautiful clothes for each season, big muffs, and outrageous fur coats.

Victim Of Dreams

Once we went out on a boat for the day, and my mother made a risqué joke and everybody laughed, she was wearing a blue sailor motif dress and would have been pushing sixty. She was forty-five when she had me, the doctors all told her not to try it. I was overdue; my Dad took her out for a big Chinese feed the night before and she always said that was what brought on the labor. I was born in St. John's in Santa Monica, California. Auntie Jean found a video she'd had made of Super 8 of my mother bringing me home. You see my parents stepping out of a car, my mother cradling me. Later on (it's not ten minutes) she's resting with me, this simian-looking, hairy thing. She's very tired, very happy.

At twelve my back was already bowed. I'd had a lot of body stuff happening at eight and ten that most people save for their forties: fallen arches, bad posture, spasms in my guts. I had leather arch supports, with slots that took leather pads for adjustment. I lost one right away and my father got mad and I had to search the goddamned school for them because they cost ten bucks each. They did nothing for my feet, the same way my back treatments did nothing for my back, and not because I hadn't the application, interest or consistency to make them work. It was to do with my actual body, something that went way beyond shape and into invisibility but was the more real for that. It was as though my body needed its defects to trigger the mind fit for it, not defective, but *defected* just enough to make its destiny possible. It worked: by thirteen and the onset of puberty I had the makings of a low grade geek, with a curved spine, flat feet and thin limbs.

I would have been fourteen. Older? I'd brought in "songs" to show someone. It doesn't matter yet. I had them in my hand (Jesus, I can see it like it was yesterday, with that grey light reflected off the lockers onto the tiles and through the air) and a few guys snatched them, hooting in mid-flight as they tried to understand what I'd written. It killed me that those ignoramuses knew the contents of my mind. I never saw those pages again. (I wrote a lot of songs, "After the Fall": "Living in a self-imposed prison after the fall.")

Across the wide flat field to school in winter, one side of my face numb from the malevolent wind that cut over solidified ponds and streams where in summer mosquitoes and skaters competed for space. In sight of the brown brick face of school, windows climbing its sides, I would already feel the thaw that would take the ice out of my pores in cold droplets. The heat engulfed me and I pulled off my gloves and coat, squashing them into my locker, anxious to seat myself and allow the warmth to work through my cheek to the bone and down my throat across my chest. The sleepiness seeped into every part of me. Everybody was half-warm and half-awake.

In winter the field was too big, the convent tucked into its borderless corner, watching and still, even in the busy air of summer when birds hung low over its grounds incubating. Closer to fall, I would walk

Victim Of Dreams

there with trepidation, unnerved by the grasshoppers and crickets bumping off my ankles and calves as they drove on, mindless of my idiotic fear. But if the grasshoppers were bad, at least by night all they did was sing loud: it was the moths that frightened me. I'd come home past midnight, sixteen or more, and come near our house with one question: Is the back light on? I told my mother, I don't know how many times, that I wanted it left off, but she'd forget and I'd find the back steps overflown by bugs circling the hazy light. I didn't want to go in, and I wanted to wake up my mother or brother even less. But fear would overmaster me and I'd be throwing small stones at my brother's screen, anticipating the infuriation it would cause.

He'd let me in, angry with disturbed sleep, and I'd pad through the kitchen and hallway until I'd hear my mother calling me. "*Jer?*" To escape my father's merciless snoring and also because she was an insomniac she slept on the couch in the living room most nights. If she slept four hours it was news. Once I thought it would be an opportunity to sleep so little, but it must have been purgatory, lying there night after dead night with thoughts of her own mother loosed by nerves and guilt.

I'd go stand over her, answering benign questions about my day. Then I'd kiss her goodnight, and I can still smell and taste the traces of face powder my lips and tongue would pick up from her soft, porous cheek. And I'd leave her there, in the dark, with spirits and demons.

"No problem" (my mother would use expressions like that, with a mocking bemusement, but at the same time acknowledge her age that made it seem funny to her at all.) My mother said she had known "homosexuals" "in her day" and they were very "sensitive". Blacks she had no problem with but she'd joke, "They sure have white teeth". She'd call someone a "miserable piece of cheese".

She was scared of cats and spiders. A cat went for her when she was three, but her fear of spiders was never explained. Once a cat came into the house and I had to chase it away; I wish I could have put her demons to flight, but the abiding mystery of any mother is not her love as much as her interior life. Creating her children's inner lives so meticulously, unconsciously or not, a mother can't afford to unload her most private feelings on her offspring. They are hidden behind knotted veils of anecdotes and intimation that burgeoning adulthood does next to nothing to unpick.

My mother suffered mentally and physically a great deal and it showed in her back, which for all its obvious broad strength was captured in round shoulders. In the figurative sense her eyes had the same sort of shape, full of a weighty sadness that seemed to drag them to you in silent interrogation, in search of the soul she knew in her heart exposed itself there but the existence of which her husband categorically denied. And her eyes were full of love of an unbearable weight and substance, desperate to enclose and contain whatever need she recognised in me to one day go far away and never

Victim Of Dreams

return for more than weeks spent in mostly unspoken communication, when affirmations of my love for her were devalued by the ticking of the invisible clock with which she timed my arrivals and inevitable departures for places and people she would never know. Time flies, but its flight is shattered and banded into pieces that install themselves as memory impossible to dislodge. Perversely, memory is often strengthened with time, not weakened, becoming more vivid with the ceaseless accretion of new, less impressive experience. My mother is now broken into those precious pieces, carried like so much bundled energy, imprinted with the delicacy and definition of a deathless dream.

Before we moved into the bungalow in Alta Vista we lived in a townhouse, and before that in a small apartment; we were there when I was two or three. I do see the living room, a brown sofa, and the refrigerator.

The townhouse - where we moved when I was four or five - I can conjure better. It was a two-storey, with a short flight of stairs to the top floor and a white handrail where I would sit and watch and listen when my Mom had guests. My bedroom, which I shared with my brother, had yellow in it, and a small walk-in closet with shelves on the left side. I remember that because when I was six and I wanted to give him a birthday present I went into it for my copy of "Green Eggs and Ham", which I wrapped in green paper and gave to him. I slept furthest from the window, and would annoy him with early morning renditions of the Beatles and Stones hits he was already collecting. My voice probably stank, but I loved burrowing under the comforter and singing to myself, proud of my retention.

I shut the door in Clyde's face on purpose, just to hurt him, the first evidence of the random meanness that would hit my first serious relationships. Feeling fundamentally powerless, I took refuge in such safe exhibitions of power, pleased with my ability to injure feelings and faces. It was the same time I reduced Ian Atwell to tears at the tail-end of an icicle-breaking competition, building up the action until to lose would be crushing. I tripped his brother Johnny on purpose too, while we were playing street hockey; I put my stick out and watched him fall into the road. I don't know if I enjoyed his pain, but my role in it shamed and edified me.

There was a stand of skinny trees there. The trees occupied a triangle of low scrub and were halfway to the new school. I criss-crossed that triangle morning and night. On the street, or by it, the one where I was six and walked preoccupied crotch-first into the wing of some stretched Sixties battle cruiser, a Plymouth or Pontiac. I was always clumsy. My father spent twenty minutes trying to show me how to make a tie and I never got it and he gave up; the same thing happened long before I could shave, labouring in vain to tie up my shoes like the big boys and girls, my bony hands letting slip first one lace and then the other, unable to work

Victim Of Dreams

them up together.

The strange thing is, I can still see myself in the mirror, trying to make a tie. His rank disapproval stung me, and I was thankful when he gave up. The dumb thing, though, is that I don't remember when or how I first shaved. Having spent so much time blooding myself on bad razors, struggling to clean the close curves of my jaw, it seems foolish to have mislaid a memory that, now I am able to keep more blood than I lose, I might summon for a perverse sense of accomplishment.

Smart kids were punching computer cards. I was punching my computer, as ever turned back in time. A misfit never suspects that things might be better in the future; the past promises the consolation of an environment more tolerant of his foibles and apparent failings. For me the future was that place where my tormentors would be older and straighter. I wanted to escape. My fear of the physical conditioned everything I ever did; the day that fat-lipped bully with the father with the garage pressed his sour puss into mine was an apotheosis of my chief dread: contact. To be touched was never less than dangerous. Hanging in the gym from the chin bar, counting myself out before the other kids, that was part of it: always knowing my strength was indiscernible, hidden in my mind, where plain girls and fellow geeks could find and respect it. That was the fuel for my arrogance and propelled me through a hundred confrontations that should have broken my nose but instead broke some muscled dope's concentration and got me out in time, fast from the scene, the perpetrator of a psychic petty crime. I never transferred thoughts, I stole them. And seeing as most of my antagonists had so few thoughts the loss of even one could trigger a minor haemorrhage, I knew I could weaken them just by picking their brains, a pickpocket with a coat lined with tags sewn in with strands of cerebellum: heads so empty that you could've grazed cattle between their ears. I had the last laugh, but it was never out loud. It was in my head, in my room. So maybe they had the edge, because when they laughed at *my* expense it was in my face.

Growing up weak in the New World the crippling thing was that it could never have been built by people like you. Jews made *money*, or coats and mufflers like my Mom's dad, but did they build log cabins or clear the north forty? Kill with their bare hands? Not Jews. They became lawyers and put the killer away. Whatever, but it was creepy being somewhere so big in every way with only a big vocabulary to stake your claim.

That very hot summer on Hogan, Apartment 10, maggots invaded the garbage room, half-born mush wiggling. I see the narrow corridor, at its end the white door. Big garbage cans, rows of them, and through and out of them to compliment the walls and halls crawling a thousand maggots in off-white. The light in the garbage room, coming through small square windows. A nineteen-Sixties room. That was the same place - building - where I sang under the covers and floated down the stairs.

Victim Of Dreams

I went to a neighbour's apartment to play and we pretended that the television dial was a bubblegum machine and the parent appeared and told me off. I was five? How can I see myself floating down the stairs from the front. It happened in the same apartment that had a back door into a small yard. *19* Hogan.

In the heat the smell sat on the cans, clouds raining soft, ugly squirm. The neighbours grouped, counter-attacked and defeated the squirming mass. Oh, I knew it made them mad. It was a new building, and for us a baby step up from the apartment. You skipped on the burning summer sidewalk to the corner store and bought a *Popsicle*. We lined up at the end of each class and whoever stood best got a candy bar. Of course the teacher made sure we all got one: I remember concentrating and receiving my reward, with luck a *Crispy Crunch*.

Inside me the memories are maggots. Leaves on the ground, matted and rotting.

Some kids had an inflatable pool in their backyard and I felt too skinny and had to wear a t-shirt in the first place to get in the thing. My arms were like sticks. I had a good time. The maze of big buildings, high lampposts and long roads, everything as new as me.

The Kusner's were a strange English couple that lived on Hogan. They had a few kids I played with a lot. I remember riding in their crappy white car. My mother made a big deal out of Mrs. Kusner's lousy cooking, picking on her "green chicken". It was well known that her cooking was a public health risk. Their apartment was a pit, too, and kids always in grimy clothes. They were nice, kind of hippies just before anybody knew what a hippy was. I can see braids, the mother's. The father had a beard. I can see these parts of them. They were parents, younger than mine, so they might still be alive. How would they describe me, how would I live in them? Everything and everybody I've forgotten - the legion of the erased - I don't have anything of them, much less wonder if they are alive. To memory, they are dead. Buried by the random selection. It reminds me of the accounts in my father's beloved books of the selections of prisoners for the ovens; the strong might survive. Memory is the same, I guess: the strongest memories survive, maybe temporarily, but there is randomness, too. Memory sometimes records life with the same insensitivity that life is lived, with zero regard to what appears central. Death is the great leveller, but memory is the rake that spreads life first, ready to be ploughed under, uniform.

We had a white car, then a bigger green one. There was a big, old-fashioned matte green water tower, but where? These are pinned to the world and cannot loosen.

Airfix soldiers I had plenty of, three thousand when I gave them to the Atwells. I painted very detailed scenes, World War 1 tanks over papier-mâché trenches. Who knows where the money came

Victim Of Dreams

from? I had six grand when I was twelve. Bought stamps. The first volume of every pulp encyclopaedia I got free and lined up on my shelf I admired them. I lived for the mail and got more than my parents.

"Another dream I remember is one from 3rd of Jan. I'm shopping for Airfix and I find myself short of bread. I leave mad and arrive at some house where there are some "Lechs" (?) waiting to fight off the Russians – shades of WW1 – that's all I can remember."

Courtice Avenue was a good place to grow up. The big field with the big hill (years later they put a decent baseball diamond in there with a high chain link fence around it and ruined it). We played soldiers there day after day. One time I hid for hours, just to capture Bruce – boy, did I piss him off! I asked him once why a bullet kills you. Bruce knew a lot of things, read sci-fi non-stop. The proverbial four-eyed straight young man, my best friend, a mentor I guess. There was something weird about the Atwells: there was *nothing* weird about them. What do you say about kids who club together to buy their parents a life-size black and white blow-up of their wedding photo for their anniversary? And the time Bill got a *Penthouse* for Christmas you'd think he had a Vegas chorus line laid naked end-to-end in his room. Elaine told me hypnotism is the Devil's work and she was right. Except you don't need the Devil to be hypnotised, you just need to tow the line.

Jeremy Gluck

'...The Atwells must think I've turned against them because I am neglecting them. I think I will for a while and use a psyche (sic) on them to see who'll break down first. I'll start today - "how long without seeing or being with an Atwell?"'

Refracted through time, of more life than I expected or knew what to do with. Sitting here now, three thousand miles from one-third of what made me, I don't have any more idea than I ever did who the phantoms are-were. Who are we when others remember us, parts and pieces of what fills the mind like dull insulation that itches like the fiberglass that I insulated the attic with for one hundred dollars and a one hour bath wouldn't budge the stuff prickling my flesh? That was one of the few things I ever did that made me feel useful to my father. It's hard to believe that I ever had a childhood. It feels careless not always to have been what I am now, grown, big, moving along rails to the one end this movie has and into which the clichés of one human history is crammed. Will the dead beloved greet me or turn me back? I hate to admit how damn much fun it's been fucking up my entire life and still coming out ahead. I always had that sense and gift, that if I could talk long enough I'd pull off anything. It works. One thing I didn't write down is one of my earliest school memories, from good old Parkwood Hills Primary, long and flat, out in the playground (warm weather, clues provided by that reliable shorthand of the Canadian climate, no heavy clothing, maybe Spring): Geoff and that girl we nicknamed Strawberry - redheaded - and Geoff

Victim Of Dreams

wasn't very bright, I was his friend or at least kind to him, but he was dumb. Anyhow, I see the tap in the brick wall and the markings on the ground, and Geoff, very clearly. No idea what was happening...does it matter? Does it *ever* matter what happened? And then I put my head on a pillow in kindergarten, nap time. A square circle of windows there, waist high. In that school I'm learning to read, five years old, at or near the front. The room was so square; I can't recall the name of the teacher. A woman. Young. I'd forgotten that I had the mumps, on the floor, pulling off scabby clumps of hair. Chicken pox, too, and measles. Endless earaches. The vaporiser and its hard green and black plastic and crust of old Vick's. Mrs. Rowan (Miss?) and her curly hair. Mrs. Gurnhill, Grade Three. Eyes magnified by big glasses, a helmet of brown hair, cardigans. A Norman Rockwell granny in waiting.

Out along Carling you came to the Experimental Farm, a field of pre-fab labs chock-full of future farming. The place had been built in the war and rather than waste it was morphed into a peacetime research place. Back then Ottawa was still small, so lost between Toronto and Montreal that almost nobody beyond the borders of the country of which it is capital knew it existed. It had a big hangover from its quasi-rural roots, for example the annual Central Canada Exhibition, an overgrown fair and farmer's market that in August drew thousands of yokels'n'locals to wheels Ferris and tractor.

Jeremy Gluck

Kenny Shepherd? He was my best friend at Parkwood Hills; six-seven we walked to school and back together every day. We'd chase each other around the small stand of trees with their fallen branches. Later he got his ear sliced by a cowboy barber, but by then I was in Alta Vista. It's incredible how much we forget. I can glimpse moments of two or three years, that's all. Life picks us up, makes us, sets us down, smashes us to pieces and reassembles us at will and we think we are living, but how can living be *pieces*? Handfuls of pieces, that's what I am; at the moment enough to feel real, whole.

Years later, Lorraine and I were in Ottawa that very cold winter (forty below in the daytime) and I revisited those places with her and saw where I was that has since disappeared into the collapsed tunnel that is the walls of memory no longer able to be retrieved, the pieces gone forever. I can't say I want them back. What we've forgotten is what we are; what we remember seems important but is just a token. The real and *important* things are consigned to the graveyards of dead memory, the war cemeteries. That feels right: what makes us is what has been deleted. The apparent is so ephemeral and trite, so green the assumption that we know ourselves when we can't even *remember* who we were and are. It comforts me to know that I am forgotten to myself already; perhaps, if I can forget even more, I can go free?

There should be poignancy to this exercise but it is more a matter of acquiring a taste for curiosity. The

Victim Of Dreams

sidewalk by the tall buildings, the pavement so hot it hurt my feet. Once I made a spider out of plasticine and scared my poor mother half to death like the time much later on Courtice Avenue when I switched the salt and pepper on April Fool's Day and my she became apoplectic with anger and worry because my father was on a low-salt diet. Me walking on his shoes and I put that in a poem one day - "Who Was That Little Boy?" - when I wanted to kill myself and the poem died but I didn't; it had my soul in it. And that's the bridge, the mode of transport, carried on my father's shoes to a dead room in a blank rental in a city I never even knew existed when I was on his shoes but in which I found Death and it forgave and saved me, Father Death sang the blues to Ginsberg but to me sang a hymn. They were so depressed half the time, my parents. But so beautiful, too, and funny.

My mother wrapping me in the covers, pretending I'm a hot dog, tickling me. A piece, in my palm. A hole in my hand I fell through to be caught by Death. How beautiful to be loved by them, even the bad times: my father crying to me the night Mom was in the asylum. I'm sorry, the way it seems to me: those without madness are without beauty. All those times, even my brother locked in his room for half a year mad with pain. My father cursing his tax return. My mother dragging herself to her inner oblivion. I can see how it was beautiful, all pieces I can gather that are like glass but don't cut. A crystal ball and chain.

Waving my memory-puppets menagerie on my

hand. *My three me's*. Paper dolls. The holes are more real than the paper. And through those holes I can see myself reflected in spaces, in emptiness, the little boy on the big shoes going...where? To England? London? A "future"? Who ever had a "future"? Pieces we had, we have, and that's all. What we forget, we are. Nothing even happened to me in my "future". I forgot, what I came here for, all I know is that I forget. I forget to live. But the pleasure comes back like a taste, a tang, acidic and soft. Old sex. Soft, old sex.

My mother was a great character hard to do justice. I can see her, at the sink at Rose Hanlon's Quebec cottage, gutting the perch we'd caught. I'd be out there alone with a fishing rod and catch a fish and not know what to do with it, whether to spare it. Hurt it. Kill it. We did those family things. Picnics by Meach Lake. Trips. Family visits. Jewish holidays. I wish I understood more about the things that created me, but by inference. Yes, we're not only what we forget, but also what is inferred by that which makes us. We're not in ourselves whole. We are the residue of what was around us. And that went into us, and became the *in-us,* the backbone, the rawness so convincing that we become "I" and die the instant death the word confers. I am left over, fashioned by the things that were around me, what was left of the Forties and Fifties (I am something left of the Fifties), my parents and brother, what they were then and had left over to make into me, that inferred me into life and then left me alone to explain me to myself before "I" became more important and the whole sorry sickness of

Victim Of Dreams

trying to justify the pieces began. So I am actually them and not myself, I am a memory of those now two parts too dead to know what a memory is where everything is permanent and we think God presides. What do they see of me? My mother, so close, and my father, far away, a universe removed. My mother, I can almost feel her breath. Has she kept me alive? Did I prove what she wanted proven? Just to be alive, after I already almost died before I ever wanted to.

She'd sing, "Would you like to swing on a star, Carry moonbeams home in a jar, And be better off than you are, Or would you rather be a mule?"

Death dislikes but respects my cheating. He makes me say and do odd things. Yet I love him. I wonder what my parents thought about my many fears. That I'd skip swimming and dampen my hair in sepia puddle water on the way home but she guessed, she told my brother I can tell when you're lying because you don't look in my eyes so he just didn't look into her eyes. She had cataracts later and saw spiders and was afraid of spiders before she saw them. Unswimming. The swimming pool piece remains shrouded in mystery: did I go too deep and almost drown or was it...a function of my fear that controlled me? And all the time the illness was incubating, saturating me molecule by molecule, the brain itself changing colour. I love the image of my brain soaking up the disease like a forlorn litmus, growing dark and heavier, removing layers of myself, the first ten years, then another ten, a final ten then before the wetness breaks the surface and drowns the part designed to find the air. And in that moment I end and I begin. A new person is born from a sac of new, unformed pieces inferred from the crucial aspect, from the madness, the sickness and the beauty of my mother's legacy, her poison, the price of her incredible and beautiful love, the ransom for my survival. The possibility of bargaining with Death, my escape from whom continued to anger that Black Master. So here I stand, still a child. I never knew what it was to be grown that didn't mean weight. My mother's arms and my father's shoes brought me here, and now I stand held and brought. This is perfect.

The useless, useless time. They showed movies in the auditorium; *2001*, *Kelly's Heroes*. The cafeteria and the lunch room in Parkwood Hills, in the basement. It's mixed up, none of it joins. The buildings seem made of air, nothing is solid. The gym, that box that dropped me from the chin bar, the stage, the staff room box. The slicing off a chunk of my thumb with a hacksaw in metalwork, blood thick droplets in my tracks to the nurse in her small box. My bad fireplace set, as twisted as I became. What I tried to do that got dropped. What I did that dropped me.

The box has been dropped: what I felt, did and didn't want, thought I knew, thought at all. More to the point the bottom has fallen out and disappeared. I dropped it out of an aeroplane and from then on every box I picked up turned to insanity. The box I carried out intact labelled "my kids" I put down safe. The others stacked themselves and became each other. I just saw a

Victim Of Dreams

tower of cardboard boxes I played with…when?

Raking the lawn. Mowing the lawn with an old manual mower, then a big power tank Ben gave my dad like he gave him everything except respect. 13 Clemow Avenue in the heart of The Glebe before boho. Big Bud's, Arthur's Place, the Mall. The old buses with their salmon pink seats and drab rails. Everything long, stretched by progress, anticipatory and old before new, squashed by oncoming acceleration. The more I look at this, it seems we're constructed from without and beyond us, filled from the outside in, poured like concrete into a mould that assembles itself: the whole world I was in poured itself into form.

The funny frozen orange juice in its cardboard tube. My father's breakfast, grapefruit, a lot of sugar. It all fell, fell, and kept falling. It came to and from and followed him to his grave. My mother and her thousand and one hang-ups, about her bridge and her hair and her weight and her back and her feet. My father, his heart attack, Doctor Malik arriving. Cy Cornblatt dying, his son Mark watching and weeping. Later my father was mad at Mark, well, disgusted at him getting his "jollies" bathing his girl cousin. Ceil was someone else he drove away, left my mother without. We're thorough.

Jeremy Gluck

About 1985, my father, Noel Gluck

Like my soldiers on their sprues; some broke off bad, most came off clean. I sat there day after day, making "set ups", arranging them in lines, painting and battling them. I'd written to Airfix in England suggesting new lines of soldiers and they wrote back with a catalogue that I wore out studying. Humbrol paints, small, light brushes and a lot of papier mache, fake grass, ten khaki tones. "If I do say so myself," as my mother would say, my dioramas were small but very well executed. I wish that I never had to change because I was happy with my soldiers, I was a general. I grew up into a small person, Reich's archetypal "little man". We know who we are. Others can see whatever they want in me but that person exists only for them. That's all you can have of me, I hold the monopoly. I don't begrudge you your "me". As my mother might have added, I'm "…no bargain".

Victim Of Dreams

I remember my father's voice when he called me "Sonny".

I swept the front walk and porch. I miss the matte silver of the screen door, the mesh and glass panels for seasons. There is more to say about the box full of boxes, about going back again and again, counting the minutes while they. Wait, it was a visit when they were both still alive and as usual it had become molasses, I was tired of the time and I knew my father didn't realise I was going that afternoon and not the next, but I let it slip and told him at the last minute. He was confused.

When it was time for me to go again my father would try to control his emotions, but when he got older he would break down. I wasn't worthy of his love. I'm not now.

My father's inferiority complex was meticulous. He worked with a guy for a while, John, and they enjoyed a brief friendship. In the war John had been in the merchant marine as a teenager and floated all night after their boat was torpedoed while his crew mates died around him in the sub-zero North Atlantic. My father exalted this. He felt inferior because he'd been too old to serve overseas; here was a real hero. Fuelled by whisky, my dad was admiring beyond the call of duty; it was both touching and damning. Without thinking about it, I can see and feel how and why my father was this man others found so complex and spiky. I don't doubt that his father was terrible to him, unloving and belittling. And his struggles to support us and find something for himself tell their own story that do not judge or enlighten but merely present him. We're all at once what we're made of and not at all its result. I don't see in my father anything he was supposed to be. Why else do we get so confused? I *know* that I am not anything they say I am. But years before when he was still sharp my mother would say he was handsome. He had a full head of hair his whole life, grey early like mine but intact. Once white, his hair stayed thick and got unruly. Van Heusen shirts he favoured, many donated by Ben, whose accountant's salary outclassed his own by magnitudes. My father had a decent wardrobe and on my early visits home I'd get one or another treasure: a period windbreaker, or the red V-neck cardigan I wore to good effect in photos. On his hair he wore pomade. He had good taste.

There aren't so many things I could say about the years later when he was getting old and his mind was failing. I wasn't there. It became harder to talk to him. I'd see him and we'd go through the same tokens of love but I'd been gone too long and nothing could change my lazy decisions. It's incredible that I never saw him buried, have never seen his grave, wasn't there when he was dying and hardly knew him anymore while he was still - despite the big twilight - living. Part of me suffers from this knowledge every day, pays for it, remembers it and pushes it away. Not so much my mother because I am too much her to not know her regardless and she has visited. I'd squandered my occasion to know my father. The last times I saw him he didn't know who I was, but in a way I never knew who he was any time. He had to die to get my

Victim Of Dreams

attention and even then it was divided. I don't feel bad about it. I just can't forgive myself.

When I started walking downtown alone (I'd make a cute little permission form for my parents to fill) I'd come out of a store and turn and walk a quarter mile in the wrong direction. Bank Street in those days boasted real relics. The Colonial Tavern. Far-fetched signs like you can't have any more, studded with singed old bulbs. Back then life, including a small city, was much more self-explanatory. We didn't need to be told what things were, they were open, like a sandwich.

Woolworth's, we would go, my mother and I, and meet Dot. I'd always have "chips and a Coke". In those days there was red leatherette and fine-looking cheap chrome. Dot was a notorious cheapskate and would wait for my mother to pay first, but they went way back, their fathers had been like brothers. Dot inherited a fortune and lived out her life with her husband Louis in a dankcoldwater walk-up apartment, her daughter became a lawyer, Louis blew the pile on golf and Dot stiffed my mother.

A cleaner would come every week, a Romanian Jew; she couldn't speak much English so my Mom would talk with her in Yiddish. She'd give her old nylons and clothes and food. My mother was an unbelievable cook. She baked almost every day. Peanut butter cookies, *mundlebroit,* lemon meringue pie, fruitcake after chocolate cake after cake. Chicken two or three times a week,

"Chinese", roasted, in soup. Any friend of mine who walked through the door got cake and cookies. My friends loved her. Virtual strangers loved her. Kids down the street converted an old hearse and they'd offer her a lift and she'd always decline with, "I'm not ready yet". They loved it. She had a lot of sayings: "No comments from the peanut gallery", "Another country heard from", "Phone the papers". She told very funny stories about her girlhood with her sisters, and her many outré moments, like the time she came home plastered with gentlemen friends and killjoy Auntie Francis appeared at the top the stairs in her curlers and gown, saying imperiously, *Father will hear about this*! Like a lot of women who could have married the earnest rich suitor, she didn't, but often reminded herself and others of the fact. Her father, who had been a cantor in *shul,* was a frustrated singer; he'd made some acetates Auntie Jean took, that my mother longed to hear again. My mother was a frustrated writer. I became a singer and writer. My grandfather died not long before I was born. I never knew my father's parents. My own parents had my brother and I when they were already pretty old for it, late thirties, mid-forties. So my parents were the age of most of my friend's grandparents, a factor in my entire childhood and upbringing. They both lived into their eighties, and that scares me, because I do not want to live into my eighties. The thought of another life as long as this one already is revolts me.

Once an aged great aunt related to me her life story. She was lying down in one of those small

Victim Of Dreams

rooms in an apartment that seemed to serve as a rehearsal space for a casket for so many seniors and someone suggested I ask her about her life. She had come from Romania and suffered and striven through an incredible gauntlet of Jew-haters and destructors to then settle in Canada, raise a family and end up the very clear, very wrinkled and authoritative old lady who told me. Sitting *shiva* for Granny I can see the apartment living room and the food, bald men, especially Uncle Hymie, whose demeanour earned him well a reputation for misery well-matched to his wife Francis, whose life seemed partly dedicated to continuing the work of her mother in destroying my own. And yet now that I am old enough I still feel nothing in common with so many of these now dead people. They knew suffering more as an external factor, from outside in. The predicament of the existential sufferer is that everything is inside out. Nowadays inside out is serviced. To my forebears, whose success was built foremost on types of precedents of survival, there was no middleman. God was vengeful. Life was hard. Even in Canada, safe from the killers, the reality of what had made them strong was never more than once-removed. Uncle Hymie was like that: one look at him and you knew.

There's Louis Levinson, Dot's husband, in his jaunty golf duds, glued to the set. My father called him all kinds of things – and my Dad knew *all* kinds of things to call people – but he was harmless. And there'd be Dot, the small-time heiress with her cheap food and clothes, too much lipstick and rouge that accentuated the boniness of her underfed features. A whole life, living on a budget imposed by some obscure imperative. I wish I'd known her in her girlhood when father and my mother were like brothers, inseparable, with their exciting and fancy new cars, many community meetings and synagogue obligations.

We want to love. We haven't got the strength. We aren't smart enough. Does God love us? He hasn't got the character.

The love of my parents is an ocean gone, an island of water. It's connected, a house built with paper. I have images of my mother before she died. The last time I saw her it was evident that she had exchanged the will to live for that to die. She looked at me, what was left of her at what she had made, and the years of loneliness and missing grandchildren and disillusionment were already cold. We didn't have the strength to talk about anything we didn't have to. I don't think that we recognised each other; we expected the feelings and memories to construct people we wanted, but were stuck with people we didn't know anymore. You go to each other, wanting something piercing. An acknowledgement through each other that whatever meaning you have to believe there is resides in this love. But in the end love betrays us; it always has nothing left to give. It comes through us, not from us. She would stand there, in her old woman's nightie, an atypical quality in her gaze, as though behind her were standing many of her selves demanding the same answer, each one jealously waiting. *Mary Esther*, *Why this?*

Victim Of Dreams

I wasn't there. She died in the night, in the bathroom, alone, my father found her body on the floor. There's a small chance she killed herself but I think life killed her.

I can remember the building and its long, grey aisles; another, strange world believing in itself. I was small in that world and saw it with love. That world was an aircraft carrier, a map on my wall: "Around the World in Eighty Days". Life is easier before you have started to live it. I didn't know what drugs my mother was on. When I was about seven I took a book of my Dad's and crayoned pages of swastikas and "Gestapo" and Scotch-taped them on my wall and he laughed but that was how I learned innocently about the murderers. I can see that room again from this angle, from the pictures on the wall on coloured jotter paper, the light lying across the wall, and a bed inside. I wonder what it was like to sleep in that room, to be me, to know nothing and enjoy the peace of the unlived.

Growing up erases all the emptiness and fills it. It was at the beginning of another school year when my mother bought me a new shirt with a bright dickey because they were in fashion, but I didn't like it much and wore it once. The fascination with details becomes compulsive: maybe if I can retrieve and assemble enough I can breathe back to life what I was, I can be small, disappear, not do the things I did and avoid becoming almost everything I now am. Being alive is a sickness and death is not the cure, but un-living maybe, winding back the shroud of years and revealing myself untouched by the build-up of what I wanted and what I thought, who loved me and the hurt inflicted and sustained.

One time I was sitting in the back of the car and balanced my new toy tiger on the top of the seat. My dad had to brake and the tiger bounced to his feet. He was mad. He got mad a lot, not much at me; though, he'd say, "That's just too bad about you, mister". My brother told me he'd started to spank me once when I was small, and I laughed at him until he gave up.

My father had five brothers and two sisters. Ros, the older sister, was a *grand dame* of her own manufacture, a big, blousy dame with a wide smile and hips. Her husband Joe was a character; at a party he might do an impromptu Cossack dance or teach magic tricks. Sonya I never met. The other brothers were the successes. Elliot the accountant, Manny the doctor. Lee worked for the CBC. The older men could look tough. I can summon up one wedding and Granny's funeral, at the funeral there were the men tearing their ties when the body was lowered. I'll never forget that ritual tearing. Then sitting *shiva,* mourning, eating, the inevitability itself a shroud. Like a lot of old men, my father took to hunting in the obituaries for friends. He outlived them in the end, the close, and the driven away, and the merely remembered. My mother held onto her friends a long time, but my father could tear them loose and did. Both my parents could be scathing about people. I think about Ben Gurofsky, who bullied everybody his whole life and ended up alone in his apartment, one child dead and the

Victim Of Dreams

other estranged. And my own father, with his love and faults, equal to me in their worth and the latter devoid of flaw, dying awfully. His father told my mother his son was "weak". I wonder what his weakness consisted of. I never met his father, who travelled the world on business, and whose second wife, Lydia, was an exotic woman of uncertain heritage but it included the Orient. She was a kind woman, still striking in old age, with a thick accent. I used to go to her house in Brockville, just down the street from the big mental hospital. My father went to a psychiatrist a few times, before I was born, but they couldn't do much. We're the way we are. Are there any real breakthroughs? How can you break through the real?

It interests me that what I've felt, been through and survived my mother also endured, only a lot more. She never knew the precise source of her affliction and a succession of tranquillisers and barbiturates must have unleashed bedlam in her. There is a darkness you can still see in, but not that one. After shock she never really emerged from it. And now I know it myself, that quality of lightless emergence. To be lost or found makes no difference in that darkness. The being has lost them. I would like to talk to her now about the mixed gift of love and sickness we share and that I never knew I had until she was gone and she never knew she gave me.

She had raw hands and green thumbs; everyone applauded her veritable crop. She swore by talking to each one with tenderness, as ever self-deprecating. Her build was legacy Slav, high cheeks and a broad brow and big bones, some jealous; my father would tease her about her Polish roots. My mother had a problem with my father's daughter in Florida, Mina. He'd been married around the wartime, had a kid, it burned out. He'd go to Florida now and then to see her, and my mother never went with him. Mina married a Filipino cook, *cordon bleu,* he had to eat a pile of rice three times a day to keep going. Dad liked Cesar a lot. I've never met him or Mina. He came back from a week there and I waited with anticipation for a good present and ended up with a dinky gold toy alligator.

Before the trip to Calgary Uncle Joe taught me stage hypnosis. I was seeing a lot of Manny's kids, and I put Paula, his youngest, into a mild trance filled with delightful suggested cartoon animals and japes. Uncle Manny, who had a big soft spot for my Mom, made me stop. Years later when I was bored and at the beginning of the end of the last Jeremy, hypnotised myself with the suggestion I would meet the chaos of myself. It took me ten minutes to drag my psyche out.

I tried when I was younger to find explanations for my father. The faggot-parasite blame-game therapist wanted more money so I quit. Meanwhile I never decided what my father's problem or chief-feature fuckup was. It's convenience that brings the "contradiction" diagnosis but I am two people so what do I know from contradiction? My very DNA cheat. He was no contradiction: We're puddles, dim and muddy. All I know is that he loved me and I

Victim Of Dreams

sure as hell loved him, and it's a shame that the last few times I saw him old age and dementia rendered him oblivious to me. After all, what did he owe this prodigal son whose star shot itself down? As for my mother, her yoke and burden was too much and I don't blame her for wanting to kill herself (if that's what she wanted to do). Everybody you talk to about suicide says the same thing, that when it feels close it isn't dramatic. The pain has already been transmuted, it's self-defence. It doesn't feel painful, but inevitable, more weather. God does not love creation so much as tolerate it and Creation is killing itself, even committing suicide, moment to moment, *neti neti.*

When it was cold-cold, I'd put on the old-fashioned gutkes *– long-johns – and bulky galoshes over my shoes, put my mother's hair dye gloves under mine, plastic bags on my feet and go into the snow. The pure air sliced itself, trees and the road cast in it.*

My father inculcated in me a loathing of the Germans. He loathed Arabs, but that was more political or maybe ideological (he'd been in the nascent Israel and was shocked by the treatment meted out to the Palestinians, so much as he would deride Arafat, it was sometimes more dutiful than vengeful); for the Germans he reserved a visceral abhorrence. The extended family of his father wound up in the furnaces, some female relative had been captured and tortured by the Gestapo. And maybe he resented fate for putting the real action that whacked the Nazis out of his reach. From the time I could thumb a book I could touch the Holocaust, browsing blurry black and whites of naked women in inspection parades, or the charred subhuman beings left in the ovens like forgotten food for a warped mediaeval lord. The titles: "The Scourge of the Swastika"; "Medical Block: Buchenwald". One particular curiosity was a frayed, worn blue-covered tome documenting German atrocities in Belgium during the First World War he'd picked up in a junk shop. Until I understood their true significance, these books enchanted me with their rare glimpses of nude women and the catching iconography of the Reich. For years I overcame my own disgust of the Germans, but deep-rooted and cosy (and – forgive me - justifiable) it returned and has never left. I still see a bunk bed and flashback to the scarecrows stacked in their huts, corded wood waiting the burning. But what seemed necessary to overcome then now I do not just tolerate but hold close. I don't want to be someone who forgives the unforgivable. What obligation can there be upon me or any of my people to forgive or forget those *animals*?

At high school maybe the worst fate was to be called to the office over the intercom, so the whole school could hear. When it was my turn, a wit snapped, "Your mother's dead!" That made Tanya snap something back and our English teacher that she liked, Mr. Mallett, snapped back, too. But the culprit was half right, because my mother *was* half dead, hauled back into the boat of life drowned with sadness.

Victim Of Dreams

You can't see back, but can *feel* it. Certain features are clear, but it's more the shadows the past casts that imprint the mind than the solidities. I know what the place looked like, but now from this remove it is more a case of what it *should* look like to me. I don't believe I was ever there, that's the problem. Am I proof that I existed? The rectangle tube, the doors with the windows, I am moving down the hallways, I am going to the office and know why/not exactly. I heard them arguing, well, my mother didn't say anything, and my father said she didn't clean any more. Didn't do anything any more. What was she supposed to do? Halfway through life with no compass. Hit the wall, absorbed into the wall, become the wall. Kill the pain, the pain kills you anyhow, the pain has the final word, the pain uses pain to speak. I learned from here before my turn came how to want to die.

In the office its shadows pretending to substance, shapes and forms, catalogued time. I am standing; they say I have to wait to be picked up by my father. He arrives and we go to the local mental hospital, which resembles Norman Bates' house but as a motel. The rooms are cavernous and the ceilings high, light entering like we're in a submarine made of building blocks. We never knew what happened and, remembering it now, I realise I've never known how my father found her and she came to be admitted. She would have been committed but she was rescued by a French-Canadian doctor who got her transferred to the Civic. I remember the wreckage of my father that night. And the hospital, I took in a copy of a fanzine

I'd been published in. My son the writer. And now *I write Mom*, she's subject/object. I'm putting her in these words like she's in the ground, wrapping her in the only things I control. I'll never know how lonely she was.

Thoughts are smoke and clear. I see her in the hospital bed, smiling with pride. I was sixteen. Whoever was there by the bed was not me now. Such insistence on living in the moment, but in what way does the past remain? Such fear of this "past". All the hidden things, the unconscious things, the menace, the dead hand of the past...what reach has it here? What I am I was, but what I was I am not. Yes, the present matters. It is as real as we can hope or expect to become. It can never be complete, nor complete us. Not even this moment can render me whole. The imagined past holds me, the believed future beckons to me, I want both, I can't remember the future or forget the past, I'm lost in a dream where my mother smiles at me, in her nightgown, in that bed.

The night my mother was admitted to the asylum my father sat and cried, asking "How much am I supposed to take?"
My mother called herself a "tough old bird". She'd say, "I'm fit to be tied", and one day she was. After shock she was never the same. When she came home she didn't recognise her clothes. Her memory refused to reassemble itself and she was often distressed at the disappearance of markers of her very identity. As she struggled to gather in the hands of her heart a semblance of her former soul

Victim Of Dreams

she came up short and became an imitation of herself. What was bruised before became beaten. The doctor gave her a positive thinking tape, she said "love" over and over - he asked her to choose a word and she chose "love" - and she was supposed to listen to it when she wanted to get sleepy. Thinking about it now, it was stupid: what good was it supposed to do her to listen to herself say "love", she *was* love. For my father it was terrible.

The house on Courtice - maybe 42, no wait, *2246* - remains clear. I loved that house. One summer it was invaded by June bugs. I stepped on my share and their black, soft shells would split, revealing whitish mush. A storm brought down an old elm and the fathers gathered to chop it up, mine included. I loved the big electrical storms you get in Ottawa in high summer, hours of sound and jagged light. I'd kneel up on the big chair by the front window and take it in. It made you glad to be small.

In the backyard the phases of my childhood and youth were staged, from the trolls to the speakers. I went back for the first time in the spring of 1979 and it was an epiphany. I had some cachet, just for leaving, turning my back on the happiest place on Earth. It was spring, the ice thins but still covers the puddles and you walk along cracking it. The water appears between the fine cracks; the ice covers the cold water in the puddles like a plastic mask, like plastic glass, like memory clouded and tough to crack. Writing about it, when everything is formed, I wish I could go back and have that time again, that metamorphosis. It seems incredible how I turned from that child into that man, but more like a descent than a climb, I don't see what I achieved, although I gained my children. I seem empty and devoid of any accrued value. Experience I often say is valuable, but it seems that experience is also voided. Trying too hard to celebrate the incidental and inevitable, jealous of the time that might have been, jealous of the self I never became that wanted to be born but that stupid "experience" - know-it-all experience! - stamped down the lid. "Experience" that promises to teach so much but eats us alive. Scavenger time, the big bird, the black bomber formation taking out life like a target. And the comfort must be concentrated in a very few items: love, children. Little can stand against the constant end.

My parents were coats and hats people. The hall cupboard with the vacuum cleaner with its beige handle reaching up my mother's coat like a lecher after a feel. And if you turned the corner, the side door, back door. I see myself washing the tyres of my father's old Plymouth and realise how normal my boyhood was. I mowed the lawn and tried not to hit the frogs. I did small gardening jobs for pocket money. But I was a misfit by destiny and design. I was exploding. Now the explosion is over and I examine the debris: the trajectory was long, steep, but doesn't seem to have thrown me as far as I wanted it to. I wanted it to throw me out of and beyond myself like an animal can run with blind energy. I got very far; I had the illusion of losing my parents and got a royal adventure. I can see myself

Victim Of Dreams

in Aunt Francis' kitchen, colouring. Probably my mother and her older sister were creating one of the feasts they built from scratch, and back before her decline my grandmother would be pitching in, her name was Ida. Ida Fleming: what a marvellous name. The beauty of the image is that it is mostly forgotten, there is nothing to contradict the glamour, the romance. The closer to us memories become, the more they snap at us with their depth of detail, making us doubt how we can be unlike how we always were and are, making a joke of our myth of life, exposed as just a pile of wood carved by the blows of coincidences masquerading with obliging sarcasm and ingenuity as truth.

1962 or so, myself at 4

Jeremy Gluck

My memories prove that I am real. I want these few key people put in a case like the one with glass in the living room with the stuff nobody else took - that was the family story, that Jean and Francis looted the legacy, and Mom never got the good stuff she'd been promised because Francis *wanted* it - that housed very fine china. The good cutlery was in the drawer. We did celebrate some high holidays and read from the Old Testament. I went to Hebrew School on and off, depending on how my father felt about it year to year. I did learn some Hebrew, but like much of my childhood, this was broken up by my father's whims. When younger I would go out in the grey light of the snowy afternoon and make angels in the snow and get soaking wet. It seems surrounded now with love. I can't illuminate this impression.

Before I was as I am I was pure, and that is the glory of those days when the sky sat on us with its Canadian winter glower, its strength of season. I want to be in the banks of snow by the driveway, the white channel, and not have to go. Before teenage dreams pulled me out of there as though by a rope I'd no choice but to grip and follow across an ocean to this place and confusion of the happy and haphazard, before the crashes. I'm not blaming anybody, but I am not the person I planned to be.

Across the street there was a couple, possibly childless, probably Eastern European; they never talked to anybody. Next door to us lived a likeable hag and her very hot daughter, Jeanette. I was in

Victim Of Dreams

their house a lot at one point. Something bad happened about the girl's boyfriend. The McConnell's were a house over, Larry and. They were Christians and had a collie, Tippy. I babysat for them from time to time. They came over once for dinner or the other way around and my father was so bored he never forgave them. Their son, Glenn, and I were close a few years. He had a retarded uncle who could have subbed for Lenny in *Of Mice and Men* and a burn mark on his hand where a hot iron had fallen on it once. Glenn wasn't very bright. After I'd left the Mounties came around to see the neighbours to check him out but he never got in anyhow. Maybe he ended up in police. His parents were so nice it was suspicious. The wife had a soft, sharp, small face and would have made a good pet. I've been trying to remember her name for months. (Small, *not* petite.)

In memory the other houses, indistinct as though smudged on, effaced, in a row, purposeless to this narrative. Across the street, next door, down the street. In the house next door to ours was an old lady who died. Her son stayed there after. I never knew either of them. Saturday afternoons Dad would come back with the "order" - the shopping for the week - filling the trunk of the car in big brown paper bags from IGA, then Loblaw's. Big tins of apple juice (I liked the blue paper label, the seam), my mother's baking supplies – fat bags of flour, baking powder, a lot of salt – cod, tins of salmon and tuna fish. I forgot to get her a birthday card and present once, and Dad tore a chunk out of me, shoved money in my hand and ordered me to go buy something.

I ran away from home - hid on the other side of the lawn - and after about a half hour got so bored I ran back in. Next time I never went back. My great friendship was with Carol Ann Elliot. Her mother, a round wreck who worked like a dog and blew her money on horoscope mags. Carol Ann's brother Kevin looked and acted like a pig, with that pug-nosed public school aspect women avoid. They'd lived in London. I wanted to lift his soldiers, lined up in his dungeon-dark bedroom. We had a fight once and I called Carol Ann "Little Miss Perfect" over and over, and she hated that. She had long brown hair, and was quite beautiful. We spent long hours playing with the Fuzzy Felt she had brought from England. Before we knew about love we had it, but we drifted when we hit our teens and after I left when she called and left a message inviting me to visit I never bothered.

An ant colony was crossing the street, hill to hill. I stomped as many as I could. Disease took out our big elm proud on the right-hand corner of the front lawn. The city replaced it with a skinny birch that must be beautiful now. The last time I saw it the house was different, me but not like me, with new people in it.

Shirley, half-breed beauty in a half-shack at the end of the street, with a fat sister and a whiskery whisky man old father. What was her last name? Her friend Maureen got knocked up. Shirley was

Victim Of Dreams

stunning, a gas station Pocahontas with a big bust and big brown eyes and long brown hair. We went to *The Aristocats* and after the show I didn't come back with her and had to call my folks and they were pissed because she'd left me behind. It was the way Ottawa gets about January, like the moon with shopping centres. The sky at night gives off its light so stingily. Ottawa then was an overgrown town. Bank Street before the boom, its ass end populated with broken-down stores, bargain dumps, and on Somerset W. the magnificent Grad's Hotel, a rube haven with a big old bulb sign. And Stephanie's, the comic shop run by the rheumy old man that Jeff and I loved. The store and the man, a wonderful place crammed with cheap comics we collected.

Canada will collapse on me; I can't hold it up anymore.

I liked my Grade 5 teacher, Mrs McCooye. I had to put up the screen, did it wrong and made a joke of it, and it shot up too fast. Why can I still remember her exact words, "That costs a small fortune!" "*Mc-coo-ee*". Black-rimmed glasses, plain pearls, period hair and pretty smile and eyes. Usually she liked me. We used LePage white glue. ("I'm ready for the glue factory," my mother would say.) Someone was sick on the bus and I pulled my turtleneck up over my nose. Mrs. McCooye told me off. That's all I can remember from that entire school year.

In Grade 6 I had Miss Taschereau, a young Englishwoman with a temper. Now you wouldn't say it as fast, but she was "homely", with mousy shoulder-length styled hair and clunky glasses, bony shoulders and dated dress sense. She never seemed happy. I think she liked us. She didn't like herself. She'd been in the New World too long without getting laid, that's my guess. That's all I can remember from that whole school year.

In Grade 7 it was Miss Williams, a classic spinster , elfin, with reddish hair; pushing seventy, I'm sure she's dead now. Miss Williams loved teaching. She started reading to us, and for a few days the class found it patronising and babyish but then inside a few weeks were in love with the late afternoon chapter she'd provide from what became an education in children's literature. Anne of Green Gables, The Wind in the Willows. I went back to see her a lot. In one way I don't like to think she is dead but in another it suits me, to think her immortalised. She wanted to slow down our childhood, to hold back the time when her kind of teaching would be a joke. Now she wouldn't last a minute with a bunch of twelve year olds, but in 1970..?

Grade 8. Redoubtable Mrs. Kennedy, a woman with no discernible personality, one of those teachers - women - Canada excels in manufacturing. She looked shorter than she was, her hair was square and face squashed through the externalised pressure of a lifetime of being straight. On top of that, she had a short voice, the syllables compacted. I'm sure she was a fine mother, and if I hadn't been such a slob, a fine teacher, too. I was

Victim Of Dreams

between best friends, scared of girls, failing everything except History, Geography and English. It was a non-year.

I was always secretive, and devious. Once I got into trouble at school for throwing snowballs at the windows. This happened on Courtice – winter wasn't winter without at least a few ground floor windows broken by snowballs and basements hockey-pucked out – but at school it meant coming home to tell the parents, and get a signature beneath a page of penitent lines. Before I wrote my lines, I told my tired father, enjoying his evening scotch, that we were looking at handwriting in class and could he please just let me have his signature at the bottom of the page? He wrote it, I added the lines and the teacher got his cock-eyed penance.

Where was I the day JFK was shot? I was five, going to the dentist's with my mother and we walked in and the women were crying. And then my mother was crying, so I remember where I was, that's how old I am. I can see the room and the seats and the faces, but faces like dark circles, no expressions but feelings.

Remembering myself, I favour a modest crane shot. Me down there looking small. Becoming bipolar, growing up two, with a cinematic flourish. Funny to think that in my better years I - who am two - could buy into "Oneness". Lorraine was the first woman to fall in love with me and discover I am made of quicksand. My heart and soul have no bottom. The elevator only goes down. Sideways, too. We can see on this graph the direct relationship between the upside down and backward line and the staggering line and the colours run into greys and the fingerprints. The "trap door in my soul": one of the phrases I coined that I pride myself on.

My mother had the same combination, and from her I take much of my madness. My father wasn't mad, but often miserable. They both seemed to be restrained by straitjackets of emotions that punished them and I had the snaps, the images, from the whole unfancy mishmash, the mean Jewish teachers to the oppressive older sister. I learned that at any time, at short notice, alliances could be dismantled. Feelings could be reallocated. I played checkers and Chinese checkers a lot with my father and in a way it was all like those games, going into spaces, occupying positions, but always temporarily. Nobody loved was above suspicion. It is hard to account all the things my father did with me. Once we went to the gallery and I mistook a fire extinguisher for a piece of modern art and he found it bemusing. How strange that none of us afflicted knew what we had. It was possible, we could have known. When I think about my mother clutching another in a series of pill bottles I feel numb.

The old National Gallery had minor masterpieces in its collection, notably my mother's favourite, Daumier's *Third Class Carriage*, a depiction of peasants huddled at the rear of a bare railway

Victim Of Dreams

carriage, one breastfeeding her babe, head bowed in what could be adoration, sorrow, or both, much the way my own mother must have regarded my brother and I as, seven years apart, we lay dying in different hospitals. The Courtice coffee table boasted a bookstand with the gorgeous book of Italian art my father bought in Rome. They took a trip to Ostia; there was a picture of my mother, posed with her head on the broken neck of an ancient statue. She was wearing her beige coat.

This examination - exhumation - should make it more real and breathless but makes it less real and more dead. Placing memories in order reveals their unreality. There's nothing real about remembering. It isn't the "clinging" of the East that drives it away and makes it trite. We don't learn from the mistakes of personal history because there aren't any. What I am is not the accrual of my mistakes any more than I am a catalogue of my triumphs. I am a recurring dream that cannot awaken from itself. If the dream is subtracted the real will be the result, and the real is not something that I want or can be ready for. The dreams - *the love lies* - make this possible. Love lies, and we listen. This is no siren song, no soliloquy, it's survival. The means to our end. I want as many lies and as much love as I can get. I am laying in supplies.

God comes first as the Devil. As temptation, torture, as Hell, God has a sense of the absurd that stretches to dead children for the sake of it. Even His own: One whole religion is based around a copiously bleeding impaled Jew, the ultimate child neglect case.

God's love is unconditional and beyond unconditional it is unable to be conditioned. What conditions can be placed on His love, He who can do as He pleases? I could take no pleasure in atheism, what a dull and righteous pursuit it must be, but God seems more and more a cipher for the fattest joker in the pack. The Devil is in the detail and God in the broad strokes, God creates a concentration camp so that the Devil can create the manifest. This is God's big favour to His errant Child: The Calculator. So my memories are nothing, they don't *add up* against the big figures. I'm not evil enough to get good. Like Burroughs said, you have to be in hell to see heaven. Once something is brought into existence it is impossible for it to be destroyed, and this may explain memory. Does God *remember*? These brainless questions suggest the sensation of rejected and inferior memory. I don't want what I remember, I want something healthier. I am not my memories until I can get better ones. I am not myself unless I can be somebody else. I free my memories, cut them loose to run into a selection of walls. The memories themselves must be rendered unconscious.

I thought I would find myself in these pictures I picked up, but it's made me inauthentic. Which of me to describe? The more I write the less interesting I am to myself. How could I live like this, fraudulent? The feeling of closing on the present, closer and closer to the idea of a person I am, to this ragtag assembly, it makes me sick. There

Victim Of Dreams

should be the sense of colliding with a great truth, an encounter with the timeless, with a core. I have no core. My memories are around me, stuffing. They're so light, there isn't enough here for a life.

It's even harder to believe that one year I sold greeting cards. Dutifully, the neighbours bought them; I crouched on the floor of my bedroom unpacking them. A Jew selling Christmas cards, does it get any funnier? I made dick and gave up on it. At that time of year there was the slush, and that's a very Canadian thing, dirty snow the colour of the four o'clock sky that has hardly been above the ground and is already resting there, scraping the day, taking off its top, letting in the night. My mother planted vegetables for a few years when we moved in. She had a year's grace, when she worked as the secretary for my father's company, those bastards who dumped him like - he loved the word - *garbage*. To my father everything was, had been, is, and would become: *garbage*. What should they do with him when he died? Throw him in the garbage. Its strange growing up with someone convinced they are garbage, that their life has been garbage, and that most things are garbage. *Waste* is not as strong a word. Too polite, it sounds like an apology, like someone is going to show up and retrain you to be not-garbage. Part of my Dad's atheist religion was this belief in garbage, except to him nothing could ever be redeemed. He believed in the things he didn't believe in.

This role model had a paradoxical beauty: at my father's knee I learned that life is garbage and I *potential* garbage. But also that his life made believable love because not even the garbage had claimed the love he felt for me. The war in his soul was total, a *krieg* for help. When I think about it, what hope did my ex-wife have of ever understanding a philosophy of love as the absence of garbage? I grew up insane, surrounded by the absurd, by beautiful weirdoes and beautiful garbage, like the garbage in that heap piled high in a godless Brazilian slum that even after more than thirty-five years I can see a girl atop the heap picking up a chicken's foot under a pitch blue sky we saw that in grade something here is how the poor, what did I know about poor? There wasn't a decent swimming pool small enough for our backyard, but I never went hungry. I took out the garbage; I never had to eat it.

My father's name was Noel Gluck; no middle name, and I don't know if the other brothers got one, but lacking one exacerbated his conviction of a loveless father. He didn't like his last name, either. I inherited this aversion and used a number of pseudonyms for different purposes. Forever masters of dissimulation, when they heard of this my parents expressed dismay. As for Granny, her portrait hang in the living room, along with my father's youthful crack at an abstract cum Cubist self-portrait when I can imagine he entertained bohemian dreams of the kind that I would inherit and expend with unforgiving élan. And there was a reasonable portrait of my mother, done around the time she married my father (April 16th, the same day as her birthday). For their honeymoon they

Victim Of Dreams

went overnight to Montreal.

Those movies we saw in high school were hit and miss. Mr Johnston - now there's a sketch - screened us *Culloden* - by the guy who made *The War Game* - which you could tell was his wet dream, give the kids reality, and it was horrible. Back then before reality war and reality death, graphic violence and sex, it was scary to see piles of twitching bodies in a muddy field. Mr Johnston liked to use the phrase "the bowels of Central Asia" like he could give history itself an enema. He was evidently insane and probably had a home life worthy of an acid trip. What can you say about a guy whose pockets were worn inside out? I hate to think of a man like that now old, maybe in his seventies, teached out, his passion to bring history to the young frustrated by the new world of instant real garbage.

I am straying into high school, which is creepy because it begins to approach the stuff I can't forget, as opposed to like to remember, and marks the time when I became fucked up irreversibly. Who amongst us can take pleasure or pride in becoming an adult? It's not like kids improve with age. They become big whatever-they-were, in my case fucked-upped. But my father, with his devotion to garbage, unwittingly prepared me well for where-we-are-now, which is a cheap and stupid world unworthy of the garbage that spawned it. My world was built on honest garbage. Now even the garbage is inferior. It isn't sad enough to be funny; it isn't sad or funny. It is garbage.

Jeremy Gluck

The more I think about it, the more I owe my Dad for teaching me the garbage religion. Go to a graveyard and behind the rotting flowers and dopey epitaphs what you have is human garbage. Life has thrown us away. We do leave behind our love, I guess. The beauty of the garbage religion is that is contains and exalts those things my father knew to be true: life cannot be trusted, when it ends it doesn't matter what happens to your corpse, God has no respect for His Creation. He called the war museum "a monument to man's stupidity" which even Mr Johnston, with his reptilian darting tongue and sartorial abortions never dealt so plain. In essence my Dad understood the tragedy of our species: we're fated to be garbage, if not our own then in some distant time that of a superior race (not that he would have thought of that). He was the most decent person I've ever known, and boy did he pay for it.

He paid by imagining his soul to be garbage. That is breathtaking religion; that is faith. The way God must deny this stupid monkey planet and its crew of deadbeats, so he denied...hold on, but then he saw God in everything but God, Bach and books, paintings, music and more music day after day. Opera, even. He saw God in His absence. He was a true Jew and I grew up not knowing who the hell I was and that was the greatest gift he could give me because pretty soon I had a burning desire to find out and the answer surprised me. Did he understand me? There is nothing about your child to understand. The hope in this life of

Victim Of Dreams

understanding anything rests in the capacity to love and not try to understand. This is not to say that things are *de facto* un-understandable. The way you feel about your child you love is as close as you will ever get to what people who deny themselves the experience call "reality". All this bullshit about loving yourself. I can't make that reach. I love my kids. If they love me then, in the final analysis, I am not garbage. Or loved garbage, and that's the best kind.

I want to begin like "What happened at that time", portentously, but I don't know what happened or what time, despite this way of tearing together what is whole. Word association for the mute. It doesn't make any sense and shreds cleverness, devices, artifice. The edge of life is a cutter; it goes through itself again and again. The images fail, the "hands catching", the "mirror" routines. Who cares who I was? If I don't know myself who else is interested? What my parents loved was real but what remembers them is counterfeit. Now I'm talking for the sake of it, to hold my ground, lying, what do I do if this can't prove they were worthwhile? I went to school, I left school. Life can be halved so easily: birth and death, marriage and divorce, happy and sad. I'm buying time and for me it's always come cheap. There was the time I wrote a horror story so convincing that at the end of it, around two in the morning, I couldn't look under the bed or leave the room. It was a good story. In it someone dreamed they heard terrible noises on the other side of their bedroom door and in the morning when they opened the door there were marks down it. And that is the map: waking up and finding the marks. I wrote so many stories..."The Heat Death of the Universe", titled after an article in a book my brother bought me, "The Index of Possibilities", a counter-cultural collection of hippie arcana. I remember its amateurish Burroughsian flourishes and an excellent ending where the audience in a movie theatre melt and flow down the aisles.

Hallowe'en night I'd grab a pillow case and hit the streets with my friends. After a few hours the case would be full and I'd go home, empty it and cover the final routes. Back in my room there would be a bounty, and I'd separate the best - Love Hearts, Fizzers - from the cheaper, bulk hard chew candies in their two-tone orange and black and white wrappers marked with black cats, owls and witches. The hard candies might still be left at Christmas. Apples got short shrift. My father didn't have any patience for the night and bought nothing and answered no trick-or-treaters. I can't remember what I dressed up as, it wouldn't have been much. We were out for hours.

I haven't said enough about my brother, and the reason is simple. To talk a lot about him will require me to betray my *faux* mystique. I am very much his creation, or maybe only half. They gave me the best of themselves, unloading themselves into me like cargo, parts of themselves escaping into me, *the innocent*. Marked least, loved best. I survived, to do what? That's what this whole exercise is for. You see, from the start I was marked to survive, because I didn't die. That was the sign, and it

Victim Of Dreams

couldn't have been plainer. Not Cain, not the Beast, just the Survivor. The little baby that could. Mind you, my brother toughed it out of intensive care, too.

So there I am - *was* - in an incubator (and now we are at the beginning, my own Genesis) dying. My father told my mother that he relived it every day of his life. Severe gastroenteritis, I couldn't eat anything, starving to death. The fact is that my brother and I were born to die. But we didn't. We were saved, by last-minute medical professionals, and by love. I cheated Death but Death cheated me back later by making me wish I was dead. I was truly one of Hesse's romantics, obsessed with the end. A shrink would have a ball with this equation, too. Let's skip that, it's too easy. There was a miracle formula that I would accept only from my father. He saved his son's life and spent the rest of his reliving it. This is what might be called a "routine burden", by which I mean what someone carries all their lives for someone else that is unsearched. He wanted me here that badly. Another question: Do human beings have souls?

I was the favourite, my mother told me; the same time she told me she and my father had done things "wrong". She told me how hard it had been being with my father, and I asked, Why did you do it? And she paused, and said, without looking at me, "I loved him, I guess."

Being the favourite was almost all advantages. I watched the family convulse from behind a protection, I was the better looking son, and would vindicate the rest of us. The only disadvantage was that I wasn't allowed to complain, but what was there to complain about? I was the favourite.

Cracker Jacks I liked special, because they had a toy in the box. When we got a box of cereal with a prize, I'd pour it into the big bowl my mother used for icing and find it and then put the cereal back.

I saw the cover of a book peel back over itself.

An old blue hardback haunted the shelves, Great War poems penned by Dad's uncle, self-published, can't recall his name. But there was another notable name in the bloodlines: James Joyce, whose Dubliners included a certain local Jew. The same. My mother's literary hero, Isaac Bashevis Singer, was the Nobel author whose regeneration of the tales of ghetto generations spellbind today. She saw him speak once in Ottawa, and with groupie reverence had a word. Wrote him a letter, and one day about a year on the reply came; she kept that letter forever.

Think I see the scrappy lot in Sydney where they - *we* - lived a few years. I'm seeing a photograph but what's the difference: my mind took a picture, developed it. It makes me happy to think I have that piece. The laboratory is gone, the technicians dead. Out of that for me came Ottawa. I ended up where they began. In the castle house my grandfather built my father suffered; by the time I came along we had the luxury of the suburbs, the

Victim Of Dreams

well-heeled Glebe had changed hands. It was the most fitting beginning for me, in that mud on that lot in that box under that maritime sky.

1980 my mother and brother David, Ottawa

When we moved to Ottawa from Sydney we stayed at my grandmother's. A splendid, old, and very beautiful house, 13 Clemow Avenue, in the Glebe that has now become the domain of wholefood wholesale and bourgeoisie café culture. It had an attic room where my brother and I slept; there were treetops right outside the window.

The next thing I see is the apartment, on the third or maybe seventh floor, and the sofa, not the one I rested on when I had earache and saw the pilot for *Star Trek,* which must have been Hogan. My brother went to the store and I gave him a dollar to get me ten packs of Batman cards but they didn't have any.

Jeremy Gluck

I can see that room clearly, possibly because there is a connection with something innocent but I'd rather not talk about it. It made that picture stick. I've no recollection of what my brother did or looked like then. Later, a few years, he came and found me in the snowstorm, I got lost waiting for him to get me from school and wandered off in my snow suit and he rescued me and I needed a warm bath; my cheeks were so raw my mother rubbed them with Vaseline. I can still recapture the knees and arms of the bigger ones as I trudged, slid and fell my way home. This would be the blue snow suit commemorated in *Snow,* written many years later in the midst of an intoxicating *deja vu*:

I walked out with the dog
into the snow
and it blew into me
stuck to me
an angel
a weapon
sticking, like memory
falling into the ground and disappearing
like a dozen memories
I would not have believed could even be
remembered
and I saw myself as I was
and did not try to understand
but saw the snow falling
disappearing into the ground
like my mother
and felt her and the snowsuit around me
the blue snowsuit

Victim Of Dreams

felt that strange kind of pleasant pain
that sharpness gives
sun was a dull yellow circle
obscured as it blew across
and I tried to hold onto these words
felt them stick and knew them safe
and how I wished the children were there
to tell my story to
my story
that disappeared into the ground
with her
and I wished you were there
to tell
I don't know why
and it blew into me
alone again
"...alone in the snow, alone at school,
from that day to this a willing fool."
Ah, do you know how it blew into me?

My father was a crack salesman who hated selling. We lived from commission to commission; I know that before I was born my parents were often poor, and that my father had held numerous nothing jobs, Fuller Brush, life insurance, like that. They never had any real security until the house in Alta Vista. When I think about how hard he worked, he seems a saint. I never made any effort I didn't want to and made a vocation of selfishness and convenience. I worked at things that made no money, sponged as necessary, and shamed my family with my lack of pragmatism and application. I had to ask my father for money once, when I was visiting right before Christmas, and as usual out of embarrassment left it to the last minute. With a sage tone and averted look, after I confessed pride as my impediment to speaking sooner, he said "You can't afford to be proud".

I pushed David into the bathtub once. His friend Pat made me cry once. His friend Dave Bagley (wore a bush hat) died in Italy and they never found his body, and Shawn Gurofsky died drunk at the wheel, and took his girlfriend with him. (It's weird thinking these corpses have zero idea what I'm saying about them.) David hung with draft-dodgers and druggies. Ben Gurofsky made me cry once, too. But then once he praised me lavishly for my capsule critique on an article in The New York Review. His wife Bertha appeared made of stone and was ridiculed for it for years until it turned out Ben had been beating her. One day she left him. The last time I ever saw him he was just old.

This list can expand. There was the cousin that went to open a hotel in the Sinai, and the beautiful *sabra* who brought us halvah. My parents would have friends over (remember the time I filled the ice cube tray with pickle juice and plastic flies?) and I'd sneak in behind the furniture and eavesdrop until they laughed me out. Like the times I'd go to bed but hide at the top the basement stairs and watch television.

Before Dad started his forlorn vigils of cheap wine and sherry and light blue movies. He would come home late and we never knew why. He denied an affair and I don't think he was having one. This self-

Victim Of Dreams

remembering is like shelling; the shells are brittle and dull, few sparkle. Life discards itself; we don't have to do a thing. It loses itself to us. Trying to bring the dead back to life is exhausting. The kinds of things that happen to us, when we read about them happening to other people, in misery memoirs, in newspapers, as great issues, they were just what happened. My father drinking and disappearing, my mother depressing, my brother drugging. Where is the scoop in that? Am I a "survivor"? Yes: of myself. They loved me, whatever else they did; I was the one who set out to hate myself.

The drug thing with my brother, the acid trip where he was in the can overnight, but I can barely remember that one. He had a grubby friend nicknamed "Frog", my father wouldn't let him in the house. First my brother moved out into the Pestalozzi, a tall project at the bottom of Rideau. He shared a house in the Glebe, too.

I don't remember much about my brother from that time, he was seven years older. He loved me deeply. When he was moving out to Pestalozzi to live with the other rebels I packaged up some tins for him and a note ending, *I love you*. He said, "Likewise", and that's how I learned what the word meant. He couldn't stand to see me cry, he'd break down himself. In every way David was too sensitive, self-destructive and my father's creation. I witnessed numerous fights, or their aftermaths; the morning his books had been torn to pieces by my father enraged by his dope use occurs. He had tremendous potential as a writer, but not persistence. He'd had a real bar mitzvah and done hard time at Hebrew school. His books, records and comics became my education. He struggled with his experience of my parents; one year there would be dark inferences of abuse, and then the next quite genuine, unsullied devotion. What I remember is the storage space in the basement of my parent's last place, where he still lives, filled with their stuff and his, boxes of it. Lifetimes of it inside three square feet or less. He went to California once (and brought back hundreds of records), and London (to visit me, my parents paid for it because, for a change, they were *worried* about him). He'd study, sandbagged in by books about self-mastery. Every damn time I'd go home I'd have to run the gauntlet: *What should we do about David*?

We all had that same love, with cracks in it. Through the cracks you could see something like tar. My brother told me that the day I was born was the happiest of his life.

Then there were the casualties. Diane's son "Bram" got hit by a car, needed a metal plate in his head and ended up a slow, hulking, handsome kid. Malka's daughter died of leukaemia. I went once to visit her, at the Civic. (The Riverside? I don't know.) She was in pain constantly and her mother was left to run around bitterly railing against the wall of deaf doctors. The end of that corridor is unambiguous, the mother coming in or out of the room, her body cast against the light like a charred corpse. Dead

Victim Of Dreams

already, for her daughter. Wide hospital-end-of-corridor windows. Her husband, Herschel (Harry) - my Dad's cousin and in that minority of relatives not blacklisted – was a millionaire who had immigrated with *nada* and become an electrical goods tycoon. He had a nice corona of bald man's hair, nice paunch and a beauty of a 'tache. His son, Mark, an erstwhile drummer, had no future that didn't consist of his father's money and his father let him have it freely, which my own Dad admired.

(I just got it: Shirley *Ashton*).

It's strange that these people were a part of my life and now I don't know when they died, or where their children are. I found out years later when Uncle Alex died. Jean may still be alive. But my father's brothers and sisters? God knows when they died. I've left myself stranded in a bottomless world, I'm hardly here, when I see the webs of love and memory others enjoy, maintain and collect, my own collection is found wanting. I disengaged and it just occurred to me that some of them, now dead, others about my age, they might have said, "*He went to London*", and that was enough. I'd removed myself, a warm shadow. Compounded by my father's refusal to keep or let anybody close, as a possible memory I soon would have died with him, prematurely. It is quite possible to be buried alive partly. I can lie on the ground, unburied alive, seeing the living.

Considering how orderly time should be, it is noteworthy how unstructured it becomes when discarded. In being dispensed it is unforgiving for its order. A year later and the seconds, months, weeks, minutes, days are cut down and intermeshed like mown grass. Nothing appears to hold anything else up. There will be a moment that is memorable - it is almost impossible to identify definitive criteria for this - and then nothing. There is a space, voided of time. It wouldn't be accurate to say that it is empty, although it was once filled. It's an absence of me, a space where I was but which my vacating has made not empty of me but a denial that I ever existed. So *I am* fractional, a part of nothing, a link fence without links that keeps in someone who might as well never have been there, and what *I am* now and live now will be consigned to the same. And the way I am writing this is a testament to the disappearance of the author. The more I write, the less there is to say, the more of myself I remember, the less I know I can find. In remembering I expected to piece myself back together but in practice am forgetting. I am reclaiming what I can, but every time I use one more memory I become a cause for conjecture.

Is there more to remember? Plenty. The big memories tell too much. I'll throw you the parts that can be played with but not fed upon. You'll get the borders. It's a paradox that at the limits of my memory I know there is a well filled with treasure. What will you do with my treasure? The paradox - irony - is that just when I might hand you myself, I withhold. This whole exercise is a farce. I have no intention of revealing what might give you me. I said in a poem: *What I reveal I conceal/What I*

Victim Of Dreams

conceal / reveal when I was lying, writing poems about lying. The detail *is* the Devil.

Dad was parking by the convenience store and the overgrown brats idling on the curb wouldn't budge. His face flushed and he spat, "Punks!" I was embarrassed. It was a wedding. We were dressed up. I can see the big room and beckoning buffet. We were in the room minutes and someone said - didn't say? - something to my father, looked at or didn't look at him, and we had to leave. David refused to. It's not hard to remember the soles of my feet frying on the sidewalk to the corner store for a chocolate Popsicle. I was sports illiterate; I went to a hockey game once with Glen and it was an ordeal of boredom. I did enjoy baseball; once my father turned up at a local diamond after school to watch my team practice.

You get: the drawers in the house. The last time I was in the house I searched in vain for the books – *The Little Prince*, *Br'er Rabbit*, Golden Wonders – of my childhood that had been given to The Salvation Army, and the toys. I read *The Velveteen Rabbit* when I was about twelve and it was the last time I felt close to my stuffed toys, retrieved some from corners and revived my need for them. I knew it was over; I would leave them behind. Next thing I knew dawn was breaking over Heathrow. The drawers were deep and the cupboards held a lot, too. They ran along the two sides of the other end of the room from the TV. Where's the auto-harp, the harmonica? The thing I remember best is the guide to Expo 67 in Montreal with its famed geodesic dome. (We went to Expo 67 and stayed with Betty Kalmanash, an imposing old friend of my mother's. One morning I saw her in another room, naked to the waist. Betty was mean to my mother on that trip, and back home my father got very angry and called her a "bull dyke".) In those days the future was still worth something, it was granted some lead time to surprise us, not like now when you can buy it between the time you wake up and go to bed. I had a decent future. I'd pay to rifle those drawers again. The whole room was fantastic. I can see the B&W TV I watched the Dolls on *Midnight Special* on and the furniture and the narrow, low windows showing the ground. There was a closet, crammed with my brother's books and magazines, a cornucopia from that time of hope built on death. I knew about Vietnam and civil rights and the blacks in the South. I missed football and hockey but I caught every liberal left *cause celebre* of a decade. But it took the Ramones to make me a revolutionary.

When I was twelve my brother bequeathed me a record player and some worn records (The Beatles' *Twist and Shout*, on Capitol, where they're jumping on the wall...and some singles...?) Later I bought a better one from Consumers Distributors (I remember when they opened, one of the first retail discounters) for about a hundred dollars, with my bar mitzvah dough. I taped egg cartons in the speakers to add guts. I joined the Record Club of Canada and built up quite a collection, Elton John I collected special. Around the same time I saw a repertory doing Jesus Christ Superstar at the Civic

Victim Of Dreams

Centre, I went with Shirley and her pals. I saw a lot of shows at the Civic Centre and then when it opened the National Arts Centre. One time I wanted an Alice Cooper ticket and couldn't line up so Mom got it for me; she had a great time talking to the minor freaks and I know they must have loved this middle-aged marvel. She had so much life in her, so much joy. The illness exults in taking that life. We didn't go to Hull much, that's the part of Ottawa across the river where the French-Canadians live. The highways went through there, and you'd see outside the city miles of tall, thin trees and areas of flash-fired desolation and then the trees again, oblivious to the adjacent waste. A bipolar wood, if you will, but that's a stupid analogy but not one I choose to revise. Ottawa then was a quarter million strong at most. Once in a while I'd go with Dad to Parliament Hill for the Changing of the Guard.

I took good care of my bedroom. I started out in the rear room right and ended up in the next one. The rear room, God, the shadows on the ceiling of the trees in the backyard; they were divine, snaking, fine-looking and right. Then one day Dave left, and I took his room.

"Small and cosy are the best words to use in describing my room. When you open the door and walk in you are most likely to bump into my bed. A large map hangs from the door along with several other pictures, etc. My bureau juts out on an angle from my bed and leaves a small area like a mountain pass through which to pass which brings

you into a small space, enclosed by a bureau on one side and a bookcase on another. The small floor is cluttered with papers as is my bookcase along with many books and boxes containing things I've collected. Papers and maps cover the walls, except for one which contains two windows. Above the bookcase is a bright green pegboard, a contrast to the white walls and ceiling. All in all my room serves the purpose."

I had my typewriter I threw at the wall. My coordination has always largely been awful (with exceptions) and, fingers smudged, I took it out on that machine, the ribbon regularly spinning out. I got fourteen percent one term in typing. He was a funny old guy, completely grey. Zachary Smith Lost in Space, without the quirk. Fucking asshole. His last name started with "v" and I don't care what it was. Nothing. He had grey hair and glasses. *Not* Mr. Voss.

A clothes closet, and two bookcases, one of which housed my comic collection, one books and binders. There was a modest chest of drawers, a bed. There was something beautiful about that house. The time my mother cried when she listened with me to *Jesus Christ Superstar*, sighing, "...what they did to Him." My mother wanted to keep her faith and go to *shul* but I hardly ever recall being in one as a family, maybe for that wedding or something.

I remember one dream; I was being chased by a monster. It was the dream of a small child. I had it

Victim Of Dreams

on Courtice, so had to be at least eight, although it was the dream of somebody younger. When we moved to Alta Vista I was put into Grade Four, Miss (Mrs.?) Conrad. She had curly hair; she liked me. I started after Easter; the day we moved I stayed at the Gurofsky's. The first friend I made was David Louis, a Chinese kid. In that class I made my first marks as a writer. One day I got to school and at lunchtime I realised I still had my slippers on, dashed back and changed.

The walls are all I can see, the inside - the halls and rooms and walls - is nothing. That was Alta Vista Public School, built when *Alta Vista* spelled progress. It's important to remember that I was born in the Fifties and my consciousness bears its imprimatur. I woke up in the Sixties, but I was branded with the Fifties. I'm that Mott song: *Born Late '58*. The world I was born into is forever passed away. The world I was born into didn't argue, nobody knew any better. The solemn wash of memory, more duty than detail. Remembering it: Retrieve, Mother, and Father. Retrieve, one, nine, five, and eight. I used to consider myself very selfish until I realised that everybody has a self, up to that point It had never occurred to me that other people exist.

Mr. Bell, our principal, humbly exuded a rectitude that died with Anzio. He was tall, with levelheaded glasses and shoes that also belonged to the Fifties, a kind man no doubt gracefully died in time to miss the deconstruction of the war age that wrought him.

Jeremy Gluck

I stole a tape recorder from a classroom, down in the basement. The room was up the hall a few doors from my locker; it didn't take a sec to stash it. Then I took it home and my father or mother noticed it and I lied and I don't think they believed me. Why have two tape recorders? At that time - thirteen - I was obsessed with tape recorders and the radio. I saw a radio-tape recorder on sale, animatedly told my father about – a "mini-deck" is how I termed it (why do I remember that, and even how he was sitting in his chair?) – and he gave me the money to buy it. I was impossibly innocent, when I look back now. I spent a lot of time listing radio stations in a notebook or diary, American stations that I would find and laboriously tune in at night when through the crystal medium of a Canadian night sky the waves rolled in regardless of distance.

It was possible then to have a real childhood, and I see now how real it was, how lucky I was to know so little. I appeared to know a great deal, talking about Marx to bemused adults, like my father a news *maven*...Insulated by the longer time and deeper divides, I was able to live day by day and not in the smashed chunks that kids now carry like panes of glass you can walk but not see through. I lived in the sunset of the old Western world, and believed in it. What do we believe in now?

My parents were innocent. For all his protestations of bitter experience, vicarious and otherwise, and with his assortment of books on the camps and crimes, my father was an innocent. My mother,

Victim Of Dreams

most certainly, with her doomed wish for *shul* and consistent happiness, was innocent. My brother…he was blameless. Once we left the Fifties it fell apart, and fell far. For me the innocence took strange and unwelcome forms. I just recalled (I almost said "let myself remember" but why dramatise, it's just that my memory stinks and it's been so long, nothing that bad happened. What makes somebody ashamed of happiness?) the insoles and the back brace. My hair.

I had a theory that my back was bent because of studying my shoes out of inferiority; stupidly I confided this to my father, whose heart it dented. I spent a lot of time wondering when exactly my back started bending: it was straight when I was born and started school. Between eight and twelve? Of course my parents tried everything: a corrective brace (an inverted girdle that made you into a cripple with good mobility); exercises (lie on the floor, convex your lower spine, stand against the wall, do the same thing); books on the head (I had enough books *in* my head; I didn't need them on top too). They got me a white contraption that strapped around your waist and drew your back up straighter. You wore it under your clothes. It was futile and uncomfortable, not to mention embarrassing. But now it seems so innocent and rather than hateful or shaming just another signifier of a time and a kind of belief that time, technology and too much money has taken. I'm not sentimental, there was a lot wrong with those days, but the more I revisit them the less I like these, so full of themselves and pretending to know everything. We are now the cowardly lions and tin men together, and it's a dangerous combination. We aren't in Kansas anymore. We aren't anywhere. *How did we live without knowing everything we were*? In those days you weren't "bullied". You were alive. It was wrong. Steve Peterson and I went to the school stamp club one night a week, took extra stamps. We smoked; when I got home I had to eat a peanut butter sandwich to disguise it. My mother guessed, but it was like a ritual. Steve was screwed up, he lived with his aged grandparents he hated and something had happened, his folks had dumped him or croaked - same thing I guess - and he had this thing about the Nazis he hard sold because I'm Jewish. He used to hurt me, but that stuff is harder to remember, maybe because nobody ever made a big deal out of it. I wasn't "bullied", I didn't have a diagnosis, I had bruises. I don't say there shouldn't be a new deal for the shit we go through. I just am glad that for me, for all it cost me, mine was swaddled in innocence.

What hurt me had no explanation or provenance. Steve would sit on and crush me, at the curb side, on a lawn. This kind of experience marked me, but I have no idea now what it did other than hurt. Humiliating, of course, but so was the brace. Who did those to me? It was messed up in some ways back then but not so cynical and all-knowing like it is now. There were still questions.

If you turned your nose up at dinner Mom would say, "How're you fixed for spit?" Or "How do you

Victim Of Dreams

like them apples?" These sayings pointed back to her youth, her teens, the late Twenties, the Depression. *"Button up your overcoat, When the wind is free, Oh, take good care of yourself, You belong to me!"* She'd say, "Bundle up"

She'd sing "A Bicycle Built for Two" and "You Must Have Been a Beautiful Baby", songs from between the wars, and recite Dorothy Parker. Nights my Dad figured she might enjoy a break we would go to La Roma or maybe a Chinese buffet; Harvey's if it was a budget outing. She'd say, "They also serve who stand and wait" – another of her inexhaustible quotations – as she hovered around the table, taking your dishes away before you'd finished. There was a period they went through when my parents wrote and called, mad about not seeing their grandchildren. I feel easy with that now. I feel close to them, and in her sickness to my mother, how sick she was, how incurable.

Sick as I am, she was sicker. I'd ask her, if I had the chance, what it was like to be sick and have me, David, my father, relying on her guts. We'd go to the home to see her mother, taste the tasteless food, encircled by the shells washed up on the filmy linoleum. When she cleaned my ears out when I was small, she'd say I was "growing potatoes in there"; I'm sure her mother said the same thing to her. She was self-denying to the point of absurdity. We saw "Cat Ballou" at the drive-in, that fabulous invention that changed a quarter-acre of asphalt into the undercarriage of the mothership for a few hours, the posts with speakers peeking in like

Spielberg ETs. "Born Free" I saw with my father at the Elgin; I remember the lion attack scene, the blood running downstream.
The two fields were the borders. At the Kilborn end a baseball diamond was prominent and over the hill and field through some trees a path came to another part where the Ryants lived. The other end, I can't remember the name of the street but Brett Pattee lived there and you could walk the streets, through the park to Alta Vista Drive and Ridgemont, or cross the field.

Brett and I hid in the tall grass and lit a fire that went out of control; somehow we extinguished it. We were playing once and he went deep in an icy pond and I got the cops; we had no idea how deep it was but in the end, to their bemusement, he just ran out. In the spring the big field would fill with baby frogs. I'd take a jar from downstairs and go into the backyard and fill it with as many insects as I could find under the stones and rocks and watch their struggle with each other and for air. I did things as clichéd as burn ants with a magnifying glass, but I never went over a frog with the lawnmower, not on purpose. I did knock down mighty hives, though, with a stick or the hose.

I loved the basement, it never lacked or lost mystery. Under the stairs there was a high pile of cobwebbed and darkening firewood, but we hardly ever used it after the first winter. There were a lot of spiders under there, and when Gibbles the hamster got out he ran under there and emerged days later emaciated and was taken back to the pet shop. A

Victim Of Dreams

lot of that happened, things going back. There was the washing machine, and a double sink and then the narrow way down to the other end where the furnace was, and the bench. Pieces of wood and my father's toolbox were down there; once I made a basic biplane and put on markings. Most interesting were the big, old shelves on the outside wall, stacked with pictures of Old Country people in the New World and framed evidence of my grandfather's status and success.

It can feel strange recalling average features of my life. My father thanking me for washing the car tyres. The broom closet in the kitchen; once my father bought my mother a new broom and his joke that it was a present fell flat when she ordered him to return it. Before her breakdown my mother was fun, *bon mots* always at the ready. She was the queen of *kibitz*, making friends at a bus stop in the time it take most people to stand at ease. She was very witty, and in her prime (which I missed...I mean her prime when I was around) could be quite risqué. Her descent into terminal depression might have started when her mother died. Ida Fleming (nee *Flumen*, but altered for convenience, like so many other immigrant surnames, by the authorities) was a formidable matriarch. She survived a pogrom in her native *shtetl* to flee at sixteen to Warsaw where she met her future spouse. These people *were* tough, they had endured centuries of persecution and kept faith with God and themselves. My mother was almost enslaved to Ida, a fact my father never forgave after it cost him his desired tenure in Los Angeles: Mom wanted

Ottawa and he caved, and took it out on her the rest of their marriage.

When "Granny" died, my mother was hit, but not as hard as my brother, in whom it triggered a half year of hermetic despair. Auntie Jean, whose very good looks and B-movie star husband (he parleyed his spaghetti Western trove into property millions) entitled her to elevated status, arrived to bury the old bird; hovering outside my brother's room, where he lay crying, she said something about Granny having had a good life. My brother: "I'm not crying for her, I'm crying for *myself*." Kind of the story of my family: we had so much to cry for about ourselves that it didn't leave a lot of time to cry for each other or anybody else. It wasn't self-pity as much as self-*piety.* To ourselves we became saints. It wasn't as sloppy or as pathetic as it sounds. Why apologise for what we were?

It's so clear in retrospect that there is next to no intentionality in what any of us do. How we live. It appears that we are deliberate and determined, and indeed these elements play a great part. But another part is devoid of anything conscious or unconscious, much less subconscious. Nor is it enough to claim that we are the products of our conditioning, which we are, but there is no point in saying it. There is nothing mysterious about our genesis nor able to be explained. We're by-products of a vacuum. Puppets with nobody holding the strings.

Through this supplemented imagination, my

Victim Of Dreams

parents are plainly as perfect and enfeebled by ignorance as I was, and in fact remain. What need has there been for knowledge? There is a rugged and stupid philosophy waiting here to be born, a synthesis of the Stoics and Gilligan's Island. We are exiles, but not *from* anything.

The Fidells, next to the Atwell's and then a long bungalow and a pretty girl who didn't play with us. Mr. Fidell with his glasses and corona of grey. Up Kilborn from the baseball diamond to Farnsworth, the new development. Charlie Truscott, halfway up Orchard, on the left from my end, we walked to school together for months. I walked past there once, years after, there was someone in the driveway that was Charlie or his brother. I didn't go up. Big John March in high school, with his ruddy cheeks. Jim Charlebois, mindless, harmless, I was walking past and he says, "Hey, Gluck, you're producing a pot!" but how could he know (he had coiled hair and freckles) it was my posture pushing out my gut? When I think about Canada I can erase what of the years affronts me. Bonna Haberman, a homely, high-spirited young Jewess. Vice-principal, name lost (S...), glasses. Snow after rain, the crust of shining ice, the jeweled pieces beneath. My happiness in the house. Falling asleep right before the end of Star Trek, for months. On at four, dinner at five. Always The World at Six, to my mother's distraction, why does the radio always have to be on when we're eating?

Do you remember, I went home after that first year and I woke up and went outside and thought the

Jeremy Gluck

streets had been widened?

Up Orchard Street to get to Alta Vista Drive. David Louis' place was on the next corner. I think that Brett lived on Park Street? Brett became a doctor. The last time I went there, the fields had been built on and lost their openness and charm. The curb where Steve told me his summer camp dirty jokes still looks good. Ottawa had gotten too big. In Canada they call autumn "the fall" because the leaves drop. We'd drive through the Gatineau October sunny afternoons, the funnel colours the road. I wonder after innocence and the puppet and innocence is a puppet, the bumbling stranger we are. I live with myself in the genuine sense, as a neighbour. All the things they have, the now-doctors and now-lawyers, the false-modest, the no-kids. I'm not them-that.

You know, when we moved to Alta Vista, the shopping centre was still open and in the winter you ran from store to store. Dunkin' Donuts across the street, Harvey's. Near the bottom of Kilborn is where Tanya lived. Rick Malloy lived further up, in a small red brick house with his adoptive parents, an older couple. We had a band in a way and during the teacher's strike rehearsed daily. Rick and I were close for years until one day I exposed his claims of a girlfriend called "Cathy" as lies; he said I didn't have any feelings, but that wasn't true: I just didn't have any feelings for those with more feelings than me. He had a job a while in a movie theatre, Capitol One, and a maroon uniform. I went back and ran into him in one of the English-style

Victim Of Dreams

pubs that were the rage for a while, he was playing folkie slots.
Don Simpson was a goofy, good looking, blonde kid, tall and athletic. I can't remember what our bond consisted of but were friends for a while, too. He called his mother "old lady" and took drugs and drank, which gave him a certain *gravitas*.

Mr Nagy was a grey-haired Hungarian emigre, who taught us French with Magyar panache and admonishments punctuated with "Gosh-oh-golly," and other hashes of benign Canadian argot. In those days there were a lot of people in town who'd fled the tanks and tenets of the Old Red World. Vlado, a skinny, brown kid from Prague whose parents had tucked him under their arms on the way out of the revolution, was one. He hated the Russians; Mr Johnston was disconcerted when he called them "Nazis", but you could you see that the burden of proof was on our teacher. Miss Toth, drama, Grade Twelve, was hot, Hungarian stock, with a rosy face, and wiry hair. We did a trust exercise and I let the girl drop and she never forgave me.

April 26, 11:41pm

And with that I cast a glance at my latest story, "The Last Bus Before the End of the World", which is shaping up admirably...History Mr. Johnston begrudgingly accepted my note, obviously a forgery and we both know it. So what? I began work in Math on ideas for my film, "I Was A Teenage Nihilist", a project in the distant future likely.

Jeremy Gluck

This looks to me like the contents of a cardboard shoe box filled with keepsakes or, better, used to hold a diorama. None of it seems real, but I know that once I lived in the box and I miss its walls and windows. The real is so much less satisfying when it is being lived. I prefer my deathless diorama in its disposable box. I'd like to carry that box and chuck it over the edge of a cliff, or else lay it under a bed. For all the pain I know that I've felt in my life, when I see the box, and I in it, I feel nothing. I am anaesthetised by the catalogue of time I've created. I am now safe, I control the past. I like who I was then, and who I am now seems a stranger. I was more real then; there was more to me, as people and places moved themselves like cardboard stand-ups that were the mainstay of so many games way back. Tape saved the stand-ups: that tape is what we call time. I feel free from the need to answer any more. I'm happy.

I shoplifted from eleven. I started out trying to lift plastic soldiers I stopped playing with when I was thirteen. Toy World, Billings Bridge Plaza, I'd be there Saturday morning like clockwork, haunting the aisles, enjoying the disapproval of the salesladies and shop dick as I cased the stock. At Treble Clef they caught me walking out with an Eric Carmen songbook, but I took off so fast the fat man in pursuit didn't stand a chance of catching me. Shoplifting seems innocent now. Petty vandalism, too.

Grade Six, Ghita Levin and Harriet Reisman were my crushes (and Kelly Leach). Laura McDonald

Victim Of Dreams

gained notoriety for making out under a table at a party; she looked and acted liked an overgrown version of Peanuts' Peppermint Pattee. Ghita would never have done that, she was a class act. Ghita - who came years earlier in the story, but what difference does that make now, with time disordered and pressed flat? - was a good-looking pubescent Jewess with shoulder-length sandy reddish hair, bangs and faultless features. Perfect composure at eleven. Her best friend had longer, darker hair. Harriet came after Laura, in high school, and was also a Jewess, and JAP. Harriet liked me, but it never got past that. I can see Ghita just inside the doorway of the classroom. Another question: Why of all the time she was in my mind, is that particular image isolated? It's like asking: Which of these people are dead?

Why don't we forget the dead/ Their voices a single note, are we living in them?/ Life gives and takes a ghost of myself/ These moments we wait for, aren't they all just cold children?/ They forget us/ Drawn by light they are blind, they don't see us anymore/ It's a sour thing, knowing them lost, for all we know to another night.

The first day of high school I'm moving up the staircase between classes and seniors are spitting down on us. It doesn't seem unreasonable.

Mr. Rayburn, sideburns and corduroy jackets, long hair, and boots on the desk. Ed Turner, trying to be your friend, the mistake a teacher must never make, and boy, did he pay. My home teacher for five years, Mrs. Seguin, a small, plain, very nasal French-Canadian woman. I wish I had anything to say about her. I can say something about Mr. McFarlane. He taught history, and like Mr. Johnston favored comic cardigans. A tall man, with a minor moustache, glasses, hard eyes and the ability to ignore an entire class for weeks at a time: "Read pages 30-45," and he sits, feet up and stares out the window and goes to the window, and sits back down and stares out, up, down. His wife worked at Ridgemont, too, and you never saw any human warmth between them. McFarlane's finest hour was when he wandered to the door of the classroom and muttered something about holding off the school (with a gun). The lockers were orange, I had a dial padlock. I must have gotten the lock from my father. Did I get money to buy it, or did he already have it? I can smell my lunch in the locker, P&B sandwiches. It was acceptable and didn't faze me too much, but I didn't like it the time that big kid pushed me up against a door and threatened me. Our teacher, Mr Voss (Dutch), tried to discipline this kid (French Canadian name, blonde hair) and got lip: his father owned a garage and he didn't need school because he'd get a job there.

I never thought in terms of jobs, I thought in terms of dreams.

I'd play in the driveway, eerie winter light enshrouding the day, and dust the pristine snow with little cones and kick, and that would be my blowing up a city. I'd lie down in the snow and get soaked. Looking back at that I feel a little, my lip is

Victim Of Dreams

heavy with emotion, because it is so *beautiful:* the light, the snow, the trees. How is it even possible that I came from that to this? From that sky to this box? How did my dream come true to form this falseness, this wrong account of who I am? I can't even write it with any accuracy, now I am angry and wondering how betrayed I've been by life. Now it's funny: life owes me nothing. Considering how little life owes me, I came out ahead big-time. I took the jackpot at Monte Carlo. It is possible for a loser to be lucky.

I wish I could see my parents again. We could have a great conversation now; I've had enough crap knocked out of me. I used to sit there day after day when they were older and wait to go home. I'd like to talk to them, but it doesn't matter if I don't. What would I say? I make a big deal out of what I've been through - as though someone forced me to want to kill myself or be obnoxious - but it was nothing. *That's* what I'd tell them: it was nothing; you didn't *do* anything to me that didn't need to be done. Insanity and insecurity, prejudice, pain, it was necessary. When I feel my mother now, it is just this that she says: *it is nothing.* Why don't we forget the dead? Maybe we need something to look forward to.

Love and best of luck Dave G Love and all God's blessings Dave God bless as always your very loving father Noel Gluck Write soon, all my love Mom As always with all my love your very aff. Father Your very loving father as always All my love and kisses Mom Love, love, love, Your old

Jeremy Gluck

Mom From your ever-lovin' Mother Love from Ma and Pa Gluck! Many kisses and love from your old Mom All my love all the time Mom love from Dad and Mom Your loving mother and father

I'm skimming hundreds of letters, most of them from my mother and father, but many, many from David, and so many friends. Thirty years ago some of them, and those the best, filled with love, excitement, parental pride, envy from friends. Envy is love, too. Handling the old envelopes, reading one after another record of disappeared time. Not feeling anything over this orgy of life past. And over those years the narrowing down to this author with diminishing love, few friends and excitement I want to speak to these many people who filled me, especially the most-loved; not just my parents, but Lorraine, and I guess teen love Tanya, too; the bit-parters and the stand-ins, the ones brought forward from Canada and loosened away with neglect of correspondence and the slow retreat into infection. How can I have been so well-populated and now exist a comparative desert? It fascinates me, to feel the shape of the gone, the tangible evidence in ten or twenty shades of ink. I want to thank these contributors. Tell those relevant, "I never stopped loving you." The most common misapprehension in life is that love ends.

Is freedom attainable? I've never had anything else. I grew up under a sky of freedom, freed myself and then chose other freedoms. I should be ashamed of myself for ever complaining. What's wrong with me is free: the chemicals in my brain that have split

Victim Of Dreams

and healed me like bones broken never to reset again whole, have enjoyed their freedom. Ideas, thoughts, dreams, and desires: all free. I am a victim of my own freedom. Too much choice. A few times I needed someone to say, *Turn back, do something different.* My very stupidity is mysterious.

My Roman soldiers the back of the comic books my brother stashed cost $1.99 on. You'd get a hundred brittle red and yellow 2-D polystyrene figures, helmets and swords. Playing with them in my bedroom, on the floor, by a chest of drawers or a night table, I don't know which. Between beds, by the lamp. I'm alone. Then it was dark grey plastic battleships. They were smaller than I expected. I'd had to wait weeks for them and was disappointed.

When I was eight I started to write my first book, a straight cop from Peanuts, which I adored - especially Snoopy (My stuffed toy with flying goggles and everything) - and I can see myself labouring over it on the floor of the living room on Courtice. I was going to send it to the Citizen. I always had big plans, the "born writer" my mother rejoiced in. I'd hatch plans for my pin money, elaborate ones, for this set and that set...

I tried to run away from the hospital. It wasn't serious, but I had digestive problems when I was a kid, maybe because of that stuff that happened when I was born. I was in there ten days, for a minor operation. I had a private room first, then a double with a kid sicker than me, his father wore a plaid shirt, they were from the sticks. I can see the room and feel that first night alone. I was frightened and it was that night or a few nights later and I was creeping up the corridor in the dark, escaping. A nurse caught me. It was a surreal week. I did a lot of drawing, in fact I had a book on air forces of the world and I spent hours with crayons copying the different markings in one of those big multi-coloured jotting pads. Before I went in they gave me a scan; using a grainy black and white monitor the doctor described what I'd had for lunch. I saw my liver. It was amazing. It comes back if you call it. Try it: call your own name.

With one memory I can recreate my life. In the same way that a single gene can recreate me, one memory can craft a simulacrum of myself. In the holographic universe, the whole is the part. One memory of mine implies them all. One memory contains and includes all my memories. My past is a point. Its span is an illusion. There is the one point, the one memory that enfolds them all that I can unfold with application.

In the hospital that I was given a jolly toy ape I became very attached to. Made from golden gelatinous plastic, it crumbled bit by bit to reveal wire inside. I called him "Maximillian". I would sit at the end of the couch in the living room with him on the arm, just us two. Eventually, predicting me, Max fell apart.

Gordy lived in the long house on the corner across from the park. His older brother, Donald, who like Gordy was freckled and wore thick glasses, sported

Victim Of Dreams

a leather jacket, attended university and was cut out for success. He'd set us history quizzes. At twelve or thirteen there wasn't much I didn't know about the First World War. Gordy was a sweet, sweet kid, and the year I got a microscope for my birthday we passed a lot of time peering at anything that would fill a slide. Once I cut myself by accident and called him right away so he could come over while the blood was fresh. It looked like a big red smudge, but we didn't care. We imagined the cells. Same as you do if you look at your skin. There's no more proof that all this stuff is in me than there is that all these memories are real. Black and white always looks more real. I don't know what's in me. I've cut deep through the unseen, and by analogy hit bone. The flesh is easy. Bone is the wall. A flesh part, with some blood, but bone bounces it back. Bone is the wall, and I've climbed it.

I wasn't precocious as much as curious. My general knowledge, impressive to this day, was made from nightly visits to the 1958 edition of the venerable World Book Encyclopaedia (maroon covers, embossed gold print, black and white pictures), a different volume of which I would leaf at random every night before bed, absorbing facts. In time like a termite I would work my way through the paperbacks and hardbacks populating the shelves. One day it was still *The Hardy Boys* and the next Greene, Orwell, Solzhenitsyn, Steinbeck and, from my brother, Kafka, Hesse and Burroughs.

My father had an undying love of literature and was fond of re-reading favourites like Proust and

Shakespeare. He loved Europe and made it there twice; once after the war when he explored ruined France before heading to Palestine to lend a hand, and again in the Seventies with Mom for a holiday in Italy, while Uncle Alex and Auntie Jean were living in Rome. Once, remarkably and predictably, he told me that if I wanted to know life and its workings and laws I had only to read Proverbs and Ecclesiastes, drilled into him the Hebrew schools of his childhood where a kid jumped out a second-storey window to evade a beating from some sadistic tutor. He had an old Bible; I think it was his own father's, an astonishing tome illustrated before craftsmanship had been corrupted. He gave it to me and I lost it.

I lived in the library. Books on the great explorers, Champlain, Frontenac and Frobisher, the ones who died mad and snow blind, the ones who had big funerals, the ones the Indians cut down. I loved them all. Some books I'd read over and over, like *The Pushcart Wars*, a wonderful story about New York street peddlers. In those days it was still necessary to have an imagination, not everything was thought for you. My imagination was enormous. It had real scope. I surrounded and assimilated ideas. I was a machine.

My stuffed animals I treasured. Every now and then – birthdays of course - I'd get another. I had a tiger I had for years I nicknamed Chubnik, a fat thing that my mother sewed buttons on to for eyes a half dozen times, I cuddled it until its stripes wore off. I can see myself in a big supermarket - almost

Victim Of Dreams

inevitably Loblaw's or IGA - and my father indulging me again. I had that toy hound that got incredibly worn but I clung to it (I almost said "doggedly") as it became bobbled and its eyes fell out. I went through a big troll phase, too, and wrote meticulous books about them, and their hero "Dorfnik". I didn't get a "big" present unless it was my birthday. Kids now would turn up their noses at what I got. One year we were at the supermarket and my folks had forgotten to buy anything special, so they picked up a toy telephone kit with the wire and tin cans, but plastic, I saw them choosing it.

When he was small my brother would say "psider", not "spider", like that: "pasghetti". A kid I knew when I was pre-kindergarten would say "Nes" for "Yes".

I got a bicycle with a red banana seat and high handlebars. I'd ride it around all the time, past Harriet's, for example. I dropped my balloon and I cried, I was a little old for that by that age, my mother was surprised. Like when I bought my big speakers with my inheritance and one blew and I cried, I was like thirteen and Mom said, You cry when someone dies, but, you know, when she died I didn't. I waited weeks for my Jolly Green Giant doll. Ninety-nine cents plus coupons. I see myself stepping off of the old-fashioned bright yellow city school bus and my mother holding the plain brown package, and the Giant, cute and simple. It's summer.

Jeremy Gluck

I was walking down Kilborn in the dark and found a purse with sixty bucks in it. I could have returned it, but I blew it on pizza. Another time I found a fancy hat in a box at a bus stop and returned it, but only got two bucks reward. At night Rick and I would wander around vandalising cars, breaking off their wing mirrors, or stand in front of living room windows and watch them watching TV. Rick and his brother Steve were adopted. Nathan Ryant, too. Ronnie Ryant looked on course for nothing' but wound up taking off to the Yukon and making it as a carpenter, a modern day pioneer.

I keep remembering the same things; I'm running out of life, how much of me is left? I'm running out of memories.

The great wintertime sky fell on the street and lent a two-dimensional aspect to the city. The woods by Billings Bridge hid the foxes and raccoons that at night would forage and clatter in our garbage cans and, startled by the porch light, stare at me with their peculiar comprehension.

My father didn't replace anything unless it needed replacing. He'd trawl record stores for classical music deletions at a buck or two, and listen to them on the weekends luxuriantly, losing himself in a *New York Review of Books*, art and the sound. I've inherited quite a few of my father's foibles and habits. I arrange things around me, moving a pen or a knife, and again. I arrange the food on my

Victim Of Dreams

plate. (Now known as Obsessive Compulsive Disorder, one more part of being alive now killed.) I wonder if he felt what I can at times, when something happens, or I am talking to someone, that outflanks my conscious defences, a gouge on my soul; fear goes through me like a cutting wire, no mark but sensation. Did he feel that? How afraid was *he* of this world? I don't know when I began chewing my fingers but soon they could be sore and ugly at the tips, bleeding sometimes. I don't know why I bit my fingers to shreds. Now, of course, there is an explanation, now there's always an explanation but actually excuse me but I don't want explanations of absolutely everything I am. I am made a self-harmer but *maybe-just-maybe my self likes being harmed it's my part in the play*. I see the explanations and they describe me perfectly and have nothing to do with me: if I can describe myself perfectly and still not have a hope in hell of explaining myself to you, what stroke of genius entitles you? I don't need "explanation". It's a lie.

My fear took many forms, but it would be difficult to enumerate them. Not because they have slipped from memory but because they have been and become a part of me now and I could no more separate them out with success than detach my arm. The types of analyses possible - personal, professional - do not begin to expunge it. To know it exists is enough and it is better not to smoke it out. I don't mind what I am. I'm o.k., you're you. And what if my self *is* harm?

Jeremy Gluck

Randall Avenue, that's the street that runs from Dave Louis's up to Alta Vista Drive.

Alan Hobson was a good friend for awhile; I remember staying over at his place, the bunk beds by the door. His older brother, Jim, was a nice guy, too. Moira Scott was Ghita's best friend, with wavy hair and a broad face and aptly would wear plaid skirts. Kelly's best friend had long brown hair and a pinched face; she's the one I thought was with Ghita. They were inseparable. I can't remember that many of them, and for sure fewer still can remember me. We exist and move in these narrow corridors created from each other's memories, tunnels, running us through each other's lives. Outside of the tunnel's the darkness of voided memory. What you can't remember lodges there, the majority of your life, a sickly white tar. White darkness. It's layered, like the seams of a coal mine, and takes energy and audacity to navigate much less profit from. In themselves the memories are devoid of value. If you can dig them out you can burn them to fuel the sense that you exist. The memories resist exploitation.

Life dies before us. Look, we are counselled to be aware and live in the present, but what choice do we have, when the memories fall like soldiers, a second from the trench and already mud. The few memories that survive attain mythic status, Burroughs' "joy and despair". Nothing else much makes the grade, but for glue we've the random selection, the pieces that need no whole. I can't be identified to myself. Others may have images, scars

Victim Of Dreams

I put there, love and hate. But mostly I am phantomic. And the ghosts are king in the darkness. They're not afraid to be dead and they don't remember anything else. They don't need memories. Ghosts don't have memories: they *are* memories.

I don't see a tunnel of light; I see a funnel of life with one very narrow end. And I'm going down it over and over. Squeezing through, losing most of my life each time, forever reduced and the same. A quantum. A bit of me is always left, and it's always a different bit, and that bit is every time one memory, and the memories don't even recognise each other, but they remember something. When I die the memories are what I am. They're small and thin enough to bed down in the darkness and hole up and never wake up, never die. They sleep. This longing for life. The memory of life, the ghosts awakening, the thin people in the heart. They stir and we begin again. Is that reincarnation? I don't believe in that. Making my mistakes once is both more elegant and economical. Where I am there won't be any future.

I inherited my father's forlorn and impotent negativity. It would have been a lot easier without it, but I don't see how it was ever going to be removed; there's a sense in which I wonder whether it is ever meant to be, this slime of mind. The line, even where crooked, must be carried forward. It's good to be misunderstood. It's ironic how the propensity of pain to mutate the mind and make us feel unhuman is what amplifies how human we are to the rest of the world.

My two best friends at that time were Mark and Evan Jones, brothers. Their father had been top secret in Iran to the Shah, taught them torture over there. Came back to a palatial split level where weekends we wasted ourselves on Brador. Mark had an incredible face with bunny pink eyelids and a narcotic gaze day and night. Evan, who suffered from a nervous disorder, was the Hyde of the act, and loved me so much he made a hobby of hurting me. We were the city freaks, the ones who succeeded at failure. I loved them both with a passion, and the revolving supporting cast attracted to their modest outcast middle class decadence, Jim and Alan, Phil, big Rob Ward and his buxom sister Joanna (who went blind), John Workman, his wife Deborah the Buddhist...the list goes on and on.

This rattle and noise in my head. Everybody that knows me thinks I'm very intelligent.

I love listening to a song you love, or have been pining after is the best feeling possible. It makes everything o.k. for a few minutes, like when I take bus journeys in the dark with my Walkman. Pins and needles up and down my back, eyes closed, stupid smile on my face, and an overwhelming feeling that everything is and will be fine. And even if it's not, it doesn't matter because very few things matter. Does it matter what I do with my life when small things make me happiest? Should I listen to others?

Victim Of Dreams

Out in the playground we made up the names of Airfix soldiers we'd bought.

Is there any real way to know what I should do? Is wanting to find what I was meant to do such a bad idea? Is believing there was something I was meant to do stupid? Is thinking that when I find it I'll know naive? Why doesn't the world scare me more when I still haven't found my place in it? Sometimes the world seems so far away.

Memories are also gravity. What we cannot remember is alone eternal.

The drawer that contained my mother's make up and sundries remained the same from house to apartment to the grave. Like memories, no matter what didn't stay the same there was a selection that did. The rooms where my parents lived before they died froze.

Old furniture and clothes, the contents of drawers, pictures on the walls, everything became still. Nothing aged nor was renewed. All of the furniture from Courtice became dated and dusty by degrees. The other room, the old, old trolley with its bottom shelf, a school photograph of her darling grandson dressed in thick dust. Untouched since my mother's hand, unable anymore to be directed by pride withdrew back into time its love. And how he treated them? How they treated him? The way the furniture was arranged in their last apartment bedroom, I remember with complete clarity. Blankets, books, the old leather files filled with years of tax return papers and insurances. Items, one by one in disuse – not able to be used - untouched as in life my father died away from the ability to use things, pick up and put down, be useful, be. It was a long decline and I missed most of it. I had my life, he had his death, a part of it should have been mine, I should have seen him buried and grieved more than with abstraction and relief, but this story - discontinuous and such as it is - comes too long before that one. I could make a lot of my suffering, if only because I can make nothing of his - or that of my mother. This is why I stay safe in the confines of childhood, when the bond was pure, and implied nothing in its breaking of my own ragtag will.

There is no secret. Don't you get it? There is no secret. Don't tell secrets. Whispering too loud, whispers long. Okay, there is no secret: That's the secret.

We're going to agree to stay in my childhood. I make this decision for you. Look,: I sang under the covers, I was cute; I gave my brother my copy of *Green Eggs and Ham* for his birthday when he was - what? - thirteen or fourteen? I don't want you to know me later, it brings on a feeling almost of panic; *I* don't want to know myself then.

I've drawn no conclusions. I wish I could see me falling asleep as a child, my mother roll and tickle me in the covers of her bed, walk on my father's shoes, be in the kitchen with my brother learning

Victim Of Dreams

the useless things, be at the bottom of Tanya's driveway, drunk at the Joneses and stoned in the line for the Rialto, cheat the movies at the multiplex, go into one after another for free, my mother cooking the endless cookies the cakes so thick and rich the stupid homemade sundaes my brother and me but the lemon meringue pie, bloody steak and perfect mashed potato, the dull streets of December before the Christian holiday, the morning without presents like the other kids, the knowing being different and the feeling of relief after the cold. You think the past is better off dead but is there *anything* about it that isn't missed? Can the snow fort on the front lawn not be missed? The first green grass of March? What about me, listening to Steve's jokes? Tell me again about the old book stores of Bank Street, sunny Saturday afternoon with my Dad, hunting for classics at a few bucks a pop. Bring back everything lost; give me my allowance blown on comics and my bar mitzvah money blown on records and stamps. I want my nights back beating a jotter with my pen, pouring stories. Reading about Champlain and LaSalle, the heroes of this boy whose man has betrayed such connections. My dreams came true and now I want back what was real before the dreams, that the dreams outgrew and ruined. I demand my mother's wit and warm, wide smile, her greying hair and eventual sadness, my father and his hated father and missed mother, my brother and his anger and five hundred records and countless books. I even want the people I forgot, didn't like, ended up hurting and got hurt by, the shallow depths, the fuckups and the few I could relate to that loved me.

Jeremy Gluck

What happened to the tall buildings of long-forgotten streets with rustic names and manicured curbs? Where's Dr. Maloney who loved my Mom, called her Mother Gluck and teased her in his sticky Mick brogue?

These tableaux of the dead and conditionally departed bemuse and enchant me and I want their population back to hold. Why can't I have afternoons lazing in the Ridgemont library impressing the homely girls, or walking home with friends? Working on the school rag, my diary, my newspaper (after months of this, I just *saw* the newspaper as though at the bottom of the pond of my life.

What was it called? "The *something* Gazette". I haven't thought of it in over a quarter century, probably more.) Why can't I be in the playground talking toys? Running through my checklist of Bancroft Tiddlers? Coming home for lunch with a friend, and my mother making something delicious, or television and grilled Kraft cheese sandwiches? They say that everything in life has its price, but from here I paid with my life to lose my life itself, and it smarts. I put in what I got ripped off. I'm sick of justifying this game and being forced to play backward Russian roulette with what I am, trying to revive what's left of me with a barrel full of what I can hardly remember I was. What's it like now to wake up in my bedroom and see my posters and my comics and my books and my chair and my desk and my drawers, all me, all filled with and bought by and read by me? Going downstairs to

Victim Of Dreams

listen to The Who and The Stooges. The Star Trek poster Paul gave me for my birthday. Two chairs, either side. I wasn't there when they moved, or when they died, but now I want back everything of me that was in that house. Yes, I want: I'm sick of compromises. I want their love.

I can't remember anything about mornings and almost nothing about bedtimes. In high school I'd often get up with just enough time to quick march the field. I remember them buying a small air conditioner for their bedroom. I remember them reading, the regular trips to the library. I pick them up like clothes, leaves, dirt.

This is like leaves on the ground, the tide line of leaves in the gutters and across the lawns, shin deep and deeper, splashing dry-wet and cool, the city dirt that is city earth on them. This is the straight, wide, long street I walked everywhere. The big (not yet bigger) cars, immigrant hives, the Salvation Army with its sheltering Indians drunk on the doorstep and falling in the new Rideau Centre, Bank Street living in the Sixties and dying in the Seventies, its trade sucked out to the edges and into the shopping centres like future museums: *this* is who we were and we were on sale, all the time. This is carrying a storm window up a ladder in October and down again in April, insulating the attic and digging out the car. This is the walls of my room.

I still remember stepping out of the door of high school that last time and thinking, "It's all a lie" or something similar. I felt so free; I did what I had to. It was an epiphany but also the beginning of this effort to discipline darkness.

My roll call runs out. I see less faces, disheartening in their pedestrian details. What's the point of remembering for the sake of it? They tell me my memory's going, but even if I knew where, I wouldn't follow. It's given me curious comforts and a sense of its undertow, but by and large it is as disappointing and unexceptional as the future, that factory of memory. I want more life, finally, just to not remember it.

Victim Of Dreams

My Second Life

"This loneliness is so beautiful. It is empty strong, senseless and unforgiving. I don't know anymore who or what I am as I melt into nothing, space, absent feelings, absent love. I inhabit an empire of radical distraction, there is nobody else here, but I am not lonely, nor alone, as legion immaterial presences lie silent on the floor."

"*I don't want to burn your cane...*", "*I want air, I must be able to breathe.*" So begins my first journal, with memories.

The last time I'd kept any kind of diary or journal...it doesn't matter but I remember leaving open a diary so Lorraine could see it, designed to hurt her, a lengthy entry ridiculing her dreams of marriage and children. One evening I threw wine glasses out the upstairs window at her when she was walking away from me to a party. She told her friends - who loved me - she left me because of my "moods". The last time she tried to talk to me I held her arm and whispered in her ear, "I hate you".

What: wake me up? Shake my shoulder. Turned my head. Roll eyes, bones jerking. Sleep on! I'm dreaming, let me sleep. You important and awake. People asleep like me. You're going to wake me up. Can't. Only God can wake me up. He's asleep? Wake God! Dreamtime talkingmall. The dog soul. Rigid unslept points, out of intelligent excuses, not outer world thinking. They call it situations, they call it forgiving thinking. Do you know how I write, know how I blew it? Then I remember...is this shadow without darkness proof I'm here? I am an island. I am no island but the sea.

I'd go to the park and sit on the swings and imagine being picked up by a spaceship, sing songs to myself, dream about going to England to be a singer. A year after I went away I came back, it was still cold, but sunny and ice was doing that cracking thing, I walked across the park and sat on the swings and I was a singer in a band in England.

I took a razor blade - back in the days when a razor blade didn't have to look like the Starship Enterprise - and cut across my lower arm four times. Lorraine looked at me and the blood and, devoid of sympathy, said, "Don't be disgusting". I loved that woman. Once we were in the wreckage of our premature love and I suggested we pray. We didn't pray.

Reading my old words, I was so young. I hadn't started to suffer.

Walking, back and forth, back and forth. Again and again and again. Same old room. Water in the walls. Wall leaving the ceiling. Looking, always eyes moving. Books I don't read. And sitting, and walking. Is it pacing? Working, not working. Filled in one day, again! Core of same thoughts. Not one knocks at this door. Should this sad house disappear? Fill in the plot, roll it over. Let the worms scramble their lazy way in cold darkness. All you worms!

Victim Of Dreams

I'd loved and lost, and loved and won. Karen was a magical elfin, cropped brunette. It was still possible to be pure, see pure.

Don't drag me into you, it's pure. Give me prayer: No, it's pure. Absolution? No, I say pure. Windows, no walls: pure.

There was Patricia the magician. I don't know what made me lie so much or so badly, it was a compulsion, a tincture of the liquid to blame for choking my goodness.

I got into a fight with God, in those days God fought clean. I got away with my love.

At the moment I am awake even before morning has opened my eyes I am playing you like a tape, again and again and again: "I love you." I smell you on my hands.

Broken chain, wet hands. One step closer to God over bodies of the not-good. Under the rain I found...hey, looks like a cigarette. Two hours later remind me, what game are we playing? Break the chain fantasyland. O, High Priestess of Suffering, what's the difference? Bleach this frame, the colours run. Egypt, glass and your sweet smile. You sweet fantasyland, Devil with nothing on. I'm in the sky, the freezing sky, ice and me, like in a dirty glass, a fury. Rip me off fantasyland...I love you fantasyland!

Always have right on your side, *my best friend*

Jeremy Gluck

Chris rejoiced in telling me, but I had no sides, just wholes pulling apart, mirror fission, division, I don't know what. I had blood on my hands, her, anything. So many sides I stopped being square. I was a square circle.

Sarah never found out about Patricia. She was a remarkable woman, with her temple and tarot and her incredible sadness. I loved her as much as I loved the women I ran from Sarah for. I loved her for letting me lie and run.

This day of endless hours: Each day one hundred hours. Each hour one hundred minutes. Each minute one hundred seconds. Each second an infinity of hours. Who am I? And where are the children? How I miss their clear-untroubled laughter! (And then I wait another hundredth and face the hundreds of thinking machines rolling unstoppable in mindless-enthused columns.)

Pale, and perfected in goodness, giving the answer I fear. Rebuked by these stupid walls, just crumpled in the corner, a balled leaf scrawled over with illegible scripts. Since before I could form words, sounds: waves on the beach closing and cold water staring up dead-eyed, so alive.

(I thought I was dead.) Nothing need be cut up here. I can hear energy in my head. My childhood is already knocking, it wants out. Tired to tag, future chasing past etc. (I even started this backward, just like my life, and now my writing is falling apart.) I decided to run away from home. So long in a big

Victim Of Dreams

body. Everybody trying to start over. Kill the child: can't recognise it in this big body. Four to fourteen that was the window. Blown ahead glued by faster air the ageing process. And then one day the gingerbread house collapsed. After last spring, that did it, night in the doorway she didn't let me in.

I decided to be bored with what can save me.

In a world I lived in when I wasn't in their house, where I was a star trooper with rights to pillage my own home, I put my hand on her back and felt me, and she felt her. I was no good at straight time and had, despite my best efforts, become unfaithful. I made it feel legitimate waking up at dawn, waiting in the kitchen to ambush my wife with 3-D mind games and then finding time to cheat. When I would go home to sleep in her bed, in her house, Helen would be afraid and angry. We had surreal, intense sex and remarkable dreams. It exhausted me.

"I wish I could remember what I say to myself. I get on one insignificant subject and blow it up into ridiculous situations, which are a lot of fun."

We sat in the grass and listened while she told me she was the "messenger" and I was the "scribe" and I swear to God we'd been together on the spaceship she saw in her dreams: our throats had been changed and, sure enough, Sam and I had sore throats. The funniest thing's she told me after awhile she had manic depression, all nervous, and whatnot, and I didn't know what she was talking about. I didn't want to shoot the "messenger" but I thought I wanted to marry her. All it took to break off the engagement was my wife riding me for twenty minutes.

My quantum marriage could appear and disappear. It would have been a winning quality in anybody else, or maybe I mean in anybody else that isn't- didn't have to be me.

One thing begins another thing begins a third thing see the pattern solids of time fabrics edged with our faces. Eyes between curves. One wedding another wedding. Warm kitchen light entering under the table flows across floor - old floor - a grey-haired man halo of white old hair he ignores me you negative hallucinated old one. Cross me out you paper, you boxes. So easy to break up, a brittle cold sweat sheet of sugar-sugar teeth. Trying to follow one line of ideas breaking out of pattern falling to a dark floor covering up patterns creating new patterns of focus denies extra thinking. The ceiling lowers to the floor.

I never could live somewhere. I did nothing to make anywhere home. I never felt at home. No capacity for ownership. I didn't belong here, didn't know how to sleep.

See it again: just *one.* We see individual part in the old movie it's our scene moment the reel moves and brushes us out of frame. One take/one minute: Never rehearsed it? The audition left behind like a coat, it never fitted but keeps packing it. Connected

Victim Of Dreams

like trains one box full of faces jerking down the line. "Can see it but not say it."

At that time I used the library again. Books, borrowed, seemed to be waiting just for me. Everything, in fact, except health, was laid in for my arrival. I ate myself, the most courteous cannibal that ever died.

I am becoming not strong but string, longer, stretching.

There was the time later, a move-out along, I told Sarah I couldn't see Sam but when she told him he became so distraught I caved and actually it was fine. I don't know what I was did to what I love. Sunday was the worst, after the kids had gone home.

You never see yourself backstage. You think it's such an accomplishment to love. The real parts of me contract in one another. I'm sick of her time. I know mine now and its clockwork movements, each shelf of trash arranged for the repetitive inspections I call my Sunday.

My discipline is to not love you. To not touch you. Not to kiss you. To not hold you. Not to need you. To not see you. Not even when I need to. Not to want you. Not to seek you. Not to miss you. Not to have you. Not to hoard you. As with all I love, my discipline is to lose you.

Sick of living an apology. All my life: "I'm sorry", my

great plea for forgiveness. And they leave because they don't want my "moods". I have my mission orders. Sure I am difficult to love. I plead "art". All my life trying to know why I am "difficult" so I say I am sorry. I feel a strange calm, strange cold. Those songs and poems, pretty word always one piece missing that space. "I'm sorry". Always pain, then destruction.

I received a phone call in the afternoon from my brother telling me my mother had died. I was devastated, I realise now, exhibiting the calm of textbook shock. I went to meditate, and experienced her presence with the sense that she was happy and liberated. I could say a great deal of the aftermath of her death.

It's a blur. It was dawn. Ten years ago. Slain diversity. Here's the church, here's the steeple, here is the good and here is the evil.

To me God was an adversary. He hid behind His son, that poor sucker point man for homo sappy-en. He mocked me with incipient madness and galled me with judgement I inferred from my mounting derangement. Always dutiful, I loved God anyhow. I was as stupid as Jesus.

Lines of numbers, lives of numbers. A book of inner construction. Spreading like oil, slow, viscous, and smooth. There's a calm, relief and release in seeing and accepting how life assumes its grid. Gambling on wisdom with solitude. All the solutions come down to a cloud. "You were the one who wanted to

Victim Of Dreams

teach?" "Yes, sir, that'd be me." Polluted virtue and reverse logic traps. Skeletal remains.

Come out grasping an area of indeterminate size characterised by you-tell-me. I dig up the bodies, dig up you, perform autopsy. That's my vocation. Other people go to work, I go inside and down like an elevator. Deeper, deeper, you are becoming sleepy...or just tired?

"Here are clues to what fate has in store for you. It indicates the type of events that tend to attract during the calendar year. For Year 2000 more than usual, you feel a desire to move forward, to improve situations, to assert your individuality, and to feeling fulfilment…Your destiny lies in areas of personal satisfaction. You desire harmony, love, companionship, and peace with people…You have a strong sense of dignity and worthiness. Your path holds possibilities for great attainment. The rewards come because of patience, service, persistence, hard work and dependability".

It's a cold place that I am entering, and the dread is for the fact that it might be a trap. I can feel my life fragmenting like ice. Rolling in the waves, collapsing upward, travelling. It's almost as though I want madness to descend. It's a creepy - sick - destiny that delivers this blow.

The two years I spent waking every morning to the same death-wish had borne its bruised fruit. I had become a black hole inside a black hole. A black asshole, maybe.

'Missing' is a slipstream, suction on the Soul, a pleasure without sensation, space unfilled, a situation: love and longing. Not loneliness. A reflection, mirrored image. Backward correct. Shed skin becomes a carpet moving, faster, blurring, crashing into light.

...with patience you drive me into a further corner. Extract my love and use it against me.
To prove Your Will stronger than mine. Your Love greater than mine. Your Grace more mysterious than I am. You use this, knowing the pain, knowing the fear we feel. You grind out of us anything useless and false. And for this I praise You, and I love You.

"A hand reaching from a dead circle..."

My internal dialogue would boil like Mother's soup, chunks surfacing, diving, dissolving, reconstituting, and reappearing. There was no statute of limitation on my lunacy. Disintegration requires no explanation: I offered none.

How do you know you're not depressed? Part of me is always depressed. Each facet, black shining, has its own depression. The many selves in darkness each in their turn and time. I feel like killing myself. It hurts. Everybody loves me but won't tell me. Who am they? I know death because I know the back of my hand. When I'm depressed every dark thing gets heavier. I release into false surrender. It gets easier to stop. It makes me cough: my chest congests, choking on heart bleed.

Victim Of Dreams

It hurts. Like a child falling over. So many fragments. Some sharpened by time cut up through mind to serve release. It's like destroying yourself for pleasure.

There was more than one of me they were loose on each other, a pack of blind dogs. It became random and bloody. I was dying butwas too alive to know it. The computer saved me, to me it was a person and to it I was a machine and it was love and I wanted to be made of wires. I'd been told that I had relatives in outer space. Fuck it; I had relatives from outer space at my Bar Mitzvah. I had the Earthsick Wish-Alien Life Disease. I did plead with my folks in the firmament. They don't collect.

We made chains. Some days I wear them. I'm not stupid. Its intelligence, reading ancient, alien script a pen in blood red ink angry ink. My smile breaks. Words are written or shouted. I go deaf. Slur life. You're wrong: That's what I think when I'm depressed. And I'm right: We're wrong. There's a rolling sensation like someone has pushed me down a steep hill. At times I like to beat myself for failure and dead dreams. A part of me rejoices. I love life but when I'm depressed that love is not requited. I get everything backwards. Sink in confusion. Escape by God.

I waited for E.T., I waited for J.C., I waited for you, for me, and for God.

It's never entirely unpleasant: I get to be a little boy. A son. Never a father. All I see is sad-eyed children. Orphans of the Soul. I stood today outside for thirty minutes and saw suffering. I love to see their suffering, not to feel alone. For a person who dislikes people I sure want to be one. I've never been in a stranger; I've only ever known myself.

To anybody who hasn't known the vindictive siren song of depression, its rhythms and whirlpooled heart are tough to imagine. Seeing in the dark? It's dark seeing.

Do you want to know what Time is like when I'm depressed? It's like me. It's like two things tearing each other apart. In its way it is creative, but don't ask me how: like making smoke with your mouth. And you don't have to do anything. You can be depressed. People like it: Depressive got nothing to prove. They want us to do but we are in the anti-Light. It's a depressive Devil in the dark, a pace of Satan, it's all the dreams of reptile Man crawling to corners.

A long time ago a friend of mine told me his good Catholic Ma said heaven and hell, if they exist at all, are down here, and I agree. What's going to be worst than Auschwitz or the gulag or Pol Pot's Zero sum? What about wanting to die for two years?

How do I know when I am depressed? I see my parents around me like hungry children. I feel alone when I'm depressed, no matter how many people are in me. I feel forgotten and have to keep reminding others to ignore me. I get excited about suffering. Pieces of me chip off. When I look in the

Victim Of Dreams

mirror I don't look in my eyes. I wait for peace; it's a mild churning. Funny thing is, it's like you could swear nothing is moving but the whole background is swirling, a sweet dance, chaos.

The less of me there was, the more I became. I fulfilled my destiny, I was endless.

It's also mediocre. Also, it may be a function of my desire to get Free, as though the Depression knows that if it can just get me close enough to the edge, I'll jump to another, new level.

I put a lot of stock in knowing the "truth", knowing "God". I was full of love forming into glittering razors arranged to despatch me in even slices to the Void.

Crucifier, your bargains disinterest me. Now stand: I saw myself as the Hand of Law, of God, move. I did not try to understand Him Who hath Given All within Morning again. Tired. What poison what antidote? Cannot save souls. Knaves all, afraid before Thee. I claim God. The page is short will find it interesting. Saw the snow falling into Transformation to blackness, average ground disappearing like my mother and witches. More pain. Trading scars for blood. You felt her, and the snow suit around me the want love, then why go looking in the blue snow suit felt that strange pleasant pain the black hearts of the damaged saints? Help you?

The winter of 1981 right through to winter 1982 was a fug of magic and black walls. The floor was black, the walls were black. I had almost nothing. I took plastic candy coffins and studded the walls with them, and then stabbed an old, blunt knife into the soft damp. Working a Castaneda mojo I summoned walls of fog, erased myself and others, kept moving. For days I would read, roll and conjure. There wasn't a part of me left peace, yet everything I am became still.

I was walking by Portobello and saw, then heard a rundown cat squeaking its death. With a hand across its face I could have accorded it mercy, but then didn't have the guts to act. Now, I think I would. That's a memory, too, that's another thing I'll not forget, will take with me to the place the squeaking stops.

"Had the first bad dream in a few years last night. Just one part where I'm in a shopping mall and I step outside and this old lady has a heart attack. She lies down, then looks up at me with this horrible face (not horrible-horrible, but unexpressable "nice" horror) and says some childish thing. All I do is scream and scream and wake up all in a sweat."

I was working in the hostel and a poor soul was deposited there by social services, very disturbed. I can't forget his look, he had been in an institution and said nothing but when the boss turned up and asked him who or what had done something to him he pointed at me with eyes as blank as they were black. I saw a man walking down Richmond Avenue with a big lobotomy scar; you could see his

Victim Of Dreams

soul was lost; he was looking for it, and would never find it. We are called to life and to death, but then the calling ends. No more voices, inside or out. A silence of light. Do I know what that light hears? How it speaks? Of course not. I am a beginner. I used to get angry when people told me I talked "philosophy" but what difference does it make?

"You created me out of your fear of abandonment. A happy child, you saw fear. It drove them away, and then you pledged to drive them away. Seeing father hating. Your last sight of him killed you. Alright, enough."

A black cube filled with screaming light emerges now to fill. It's like a life. Unconscious of birth, afraid of death. Rising up levels to engulf lies. Even the cube cares. Its edges exist within your heart centre. Being punched out from the inside. All this destruction must cease. Everything, until main eyes stick into myself tight, main, long, grows nothing but victims-myself. Eyes stick and metamorphosis eats and dreams, hiding dark tongues and arms, organs and victims left but left, biding time, biding *victims*.

I'd endured loneliness that crushed like a vice; I'd climb the stairs to my somebody-else's bedroom at eleven and think, I made it again. I'd breathed in a vacuum. Sleep saved me.

It began before dawn, in the dark, alone in a narrow bed, a narrow mind. The light did not arrive for too long. In the darkness, I felt visceral fear, of the aloneness; the same aloneness that, at other times, I celebrate and draw on for strength. Thoughts, messy and soft with sleepless heaviness, hounded and pursued and cornered me, always the same thoughts, images - love, sex - repeating like a rifle. And it went on all day, well, until two o'clock, when I decided again to live. I know what this periodical visitation of pain *is* simply a dying within for want of love, affection and physical warmth from another being, from a woman - a girl - no, a woman. It is like dying from the inside out, it cries without being heard and hammers like hail in the heart, crashing around blind with self-pity, longing and confused anger. The essential human right must be: *the right to love*.

I remember the toboggan rides in the dead of winter, sliding to the trees, the shouting. Clinging to the one in front, jumping off. Now there was nobody to cling to and nobody in front. The same trees that have harboured me had closed their arms to me. I was no longer alone.

Face to the glyphs, I am supremely happy. I can still feel the pain but it doesn't hurt. It's otherworldly, this distorted happiness. It's merry masks wearing each other, tone and colour and life. It's a dirty part of heaven that has its mud scraped off. A pocket benediction. Where to from here? My life is spinning out of its former tame orbit into an outer belt of minor chaos. The heart aches but not beyond bearing; far from it; even the pain's pleasure. I am breaking up, long-awaited shattering, the displacement of lies. Reckless and

Victim Of Dreams

weird, scratched and scarred, chunks torn and chewed off...missing, wanting, loving, not loving, waiting, worrying, tripping. A nobody trying to be a somebody will become anybody and thus be lost. All positions have no place.

I walked in the woods, thinking, "I love you, Patricia". Where is she now, where am I? You see, the nights then – when we rode the toboggans – were very clear. The abandoned air base and its long hill sheeted with ice. Phil got a concussion broke something. We were crazy to do it, the road was close, and there was no way to stop on the ice. It went down a few hundred feet. And underneath the ice was the frozen ground. And underneath my skin was the frozen blood. I wanted to be warm.

I am a sharp and broken piece of what I was, wearing down with friction, with speed. I don't know who I am, Sarah is, anybody is, I don't want to. Let them live, flourish and die: A prayer in light, a sleep in dream, a word unused. I love this *riot* of energy more than anything, any other living thing.

This "riot of energy" degenerated into looting, the last healthy parts of me broken by a star falling from orbit. I was science fiction, I was Death.

What of the bliss of death, of knowing the heart collected in its very disintegration? You can get to happiness through unhappiness; it's a high risk, high contrast business and it works better than you'd expect. For six hours I barely moved, just sat and saw what I wanted to, a catalogue of self-pity and collapse worthy of a Gothic dime novel: drama, but without the plot. The usual feelings rode over me, thinking about death, which I love to think about...few people are fond of death, but I sure am...it is a song I am learning and when I need it I'll have it ready, to sing, when I cross The Western Lands. I am privileged now to be aware of my forgetting. I can feel myself forgetting, and I don't think I've ever experienced that before: to do this, you must remember intensely, with passion and intent, with a view to self-damaging imprinting, but you find that as you focus on love - and what the hell else is there to focus on? - the love itself, with its mysterious and active living will emerges distinct and overcomes all the negative energy and delivers you to a plateau of emotional equanimity. Love will find a use for you; make you a vessel, a receptor, a spectator. A message. There's nothing in my way. I can move in all directions with freedom.

But there was something in my way. I had to go through myself first. And no amount of false certainty or New Age soap flakery was going to provide the lift-off necessary. To get through myself I had to take myself with me. I was never going to get off the hook just with "love".

At the moment I choose to - must - rest static and unexpressed. Emptying, building. Waiting, wanting. I forgive myself desire...it is a bondage, but it serves the purpose of making us sticky to the 3-D. It keeps us attached to the surface, in more ways than one. It makes us stay. Death is the end of desire and the beginning of satisfaction. Rest. How

Victim Of Dreams

I long for it at times, but I also love being alive. Is it a balancing act? I could make my life end - will it - but I choose not to. I came back here for a reason, and I know that in one way it has been a disastrous experiment... The truth can be insufferably pedantic. It stops and starts and we get trapped between positions, neither true nor untrue, drifters. I love the drift. A seasonal change. I want to fly, and I will, from this body and look down upon this fractured life and see it of a piece and rejoice in forgetting it. I am exploded...by an agency or will beyond me, and liberated in chaos. I fear not the night, nor myself. I declare for blind progress, for empty afternoons, for waste and impulse and sheer stupid puppy love. I haven't grown up a bit, I am still singing on a swing looking out over Time and talking to it.

The day I came back from Canada and they were gone. I broke a chair, or table - I forget which - and then sat on the stairs and tried to cry, but it seemed derisory.

I'm lonely, I feel like I'm dying. Time walking on my back, face pressed into earth. A searching look into deep six wondering where these people who love me are. I wish it would stop; every time I think it does it doesn't. It's behind me like a gun. Made my whole life feel a lot bigger. Spread thin, folded it and then corroded it. I don't mind, I am used to being used. I am used to being. I am writing this to fill the space threatening to rip me open and smear me from here to another minute. Temptation, rehabilitation, I don't need it I'm pure enough, I can die, I'm ready.

I did writing for an erstwhile therapist whose routines brought me nothing but the two key images of my inborn nemesis: the Black Cube and the Black Magnet.

"We're loving you so that you can die."

God, definitely.

"Interpolated in space and time to wreck man."

Memory requires time and fatally I had enough of the latter to swell the former.

"I am the cube, the dead cube, the master cube, the cube, I feel what you feel, I fill you with pain, a spiteful cube."

God, definitely.

A polar light system, an alien device. There is no necessity to understand the cube: It understands itself. Who knows its reasons? I can't bear to write these words. The cube makes me tired. Awareness of decay: I want to be with the insane, mad people - decayed angels.

"*You...*" (Voice of my father).

I hear screaming in my head, often my inner scream.

Victim Of Dreams

("A scream is worth a thousand words.")

It's passed down like lead.

Unless you can find in anything an extreme value, which makes possible at its very extreme scope for insanity, that thing is of no real value; not because the world is insane, but because the world is chaotic.

This laughable and disposable creature, reaching for redemption. Beaten back a thousand times by the disease of my mind. Mine, the body they walk over - this wrecked corpse in lime. Feeling sorry for myself the way one examines a deep wound, probing for muscle where there is only bone. The motor power of standing still, the self-forgiveness of idiot good intention. I am brought here as a sacrifice and drink from a bowl of Mother's soup salted with tears. I choose and handle a memory. Memory, our pricking of Death: a defence against the welcome annihilation, dropping memories like coins rolled into the gutter of unseen forces.

The day I left the gas on I called he and, read my new poem, Who Was That Little Boy? *She cried; I did. It's amazing how when you don't fuck each other any more you can cry together so much. Was it? "Death smiled and looked to one side," another page of my legend, my cycle of death. Death isn't lazy, just resigned. Death knows humility because it spends so much time waiting. I smoked and slept to get through the hours there. I pissed out the door and watched the clock like a terminal patient, not sure if I wanted another minute or not. Anyhow, I got it, and I made the next reprieve. She'd gone to the States to scout some asshole Catholic academic and it went bad. When she got back I was waiting and I took what I could get, which was the usual nothing.*

I understand no language but speak because without it without words I hate them myself my curse until God dissolves me in His presence I remain poisoned by love, bleeding love deep, dark red, sticking love feral love shining anger like a forest animal eyes disturbed by light.

I got lost on my way to myself, that's how stupid I am. I believed in everything sooner or later. Karma: I deserve this. The thing where you know everything before you're even born and fuck yourself on purpose: I planned this. Fate: I didn't have anything to do with this. Destiny: I was always going to do this. Predestination: Destiny, but stupider. Astrology: I'm not that fucked up!

'In and of itself' and such phrases and formulations: Everybody that expects to be important will be disappointed. When I'd come home again to the lie we meditated and Sarah saw the Light, in fact it literally welcomed her. In the dream of love, again recapturing what she didn't want or have any use for, she let it touch her. Within weeks it was the same old same old, anti-depressants that didn't work for me, the straight time clock ticking her blood for her. We are what we are, as night follows night. We had no hope whatsoever of creating

Victim Of Dreams

anything other than a caricature of what had been, when the babies were young and we were not stained with each other like rags. A literal description of the ills that befell me attempting to oblige the lie is not necessary here. I betrayed myself again, it had become habitual, all I knew was how to throw myself at myself and take the hit. I didn't want anything she wanted; she didn't want me or anything I am. It played out like the kind of very bad novel lonely ladies read, but without the romance or the exciting climax and come to think of it without any climaxes.

Time does not provide light.

I slept one hundred hours, I worked one thousand years. Laughing time, preferring to send its messages by night watches over us as the pain of living commuted to space without ending disappears. Laughing time, in its narcissistic glory looks askance and makes obscene faces at our trials. Dead pages turn, and words faded but legible suggest paths out of this damnable vice. To push so hard and split the screws drilling through our minds. So sleep sweetly, dear child of God. The mystery is why I am still the same wrecked ship on the same blind reef after six hundred voyages I am still against the wind and bent with cold, I'm not even old, I feel young, I feel old, I've never been young, when I was a child I was old and now I just want to be a child.

Anybody who thinks there is not evil in this world is

in for a big surprise. Hell is the Parasite. The Master Parasite. On our shoulders like a marine rifle, seeped into bruises. I woke up smoking listening to television. I've known Bliss, The White River. Father, forgive them, they know what they do. Jesus loves a liar: Judas.

I turned myself into the authorities.

Carrying the past out of a burning building, smoke as thought. Funny how time provides so little light, hallway you can almost see edges, corners, but where is fact? It slips from grasp like heat. Effort to reach back into psyche dry and old will result in pain. Get your answers prefabricated: a thousand helpful experts arrive armed with lonely words they create for conventions to keep company. Fate, Destiny, Luck, even God and His whole corporate structure, cannot protect you from "need to know basis". Curious about the past, interleaved with love, thin and wafered, a delicacy served shoved-down-the-throat in a five dollar seat Saturday afternoon at the Rialto, horror triple bill, every movie stacked like time, you were maybe twelve, no, maybe sixteen, no, but it cost a buck, make that one-fifty: see what I mean - no edges.

I'd made my pilgrimage to the limit and it had torn half of me out and spat it where I could never get it back. I was happy to be alive, lucky to be.

Pushed through a doorway from behind, the desire to use the past. It tramples you, give it a chance to

Victim Of Dreams

get out. No qualifications: what qualifications can the past have? Its time has gone, literally. So it aches, empty and cantankerous, using cigarettes for a clock, counting down in nicotine, calculating the main chance: will he look back? One look back you're shot through that doorway your head revolving. Time as the past, like nails and hair, has no nerve endings: you let it grow in eventually and shears away so-called Future; you cut it, it grows back. Its own numb longing: the past.

I became unafraid. But the illness would not grant a true freedom: everything must avenge every other thing.

Factor in so-called *Love* and start the party. Everything built on something else dead so no wonder we have eight colours, a brain ninety per cent dead and church with three nails for collateral. When they came for Jesus He should have told the truth: No way am I going down for this piss-poor excuse for a species. On Alpha Centauri they have two heads apiece and they both think. But, no, His brief from Central Casting was simple: We're into this for two thousand years top profits. He threw the fight good. He could have come off the cross at Calvary and laid them out like slabs the ditches of Belsen but that would be cheap: they wanna '*suffer*'.

Karen-time at the real beginning of the superdowners. Escape became telling myself for three days solid, "I'm dead".

Now everybody's guilty, bar the weekend warriors and the usual cartels. The longest murder hunt in history: "Who killed J.C.?" Evidence has it's the fucking Jews – again! – but ain't that too pat? Until they gave them guns the Jews wouldn't hurt a fly. Nah. It's more serious. Must have been a conspiracy back projection from the Vatican can you imagine it 200(0-9) and they can control time run it like a 8mm flick, a home planet movie, so to speak. And there's enough past to spit out a cult the size of all get out.

So they set up the Son of God, they set up the Jews – again! So hard to unglue the past. How I wish I could crawl from it one person, not this corrugated shyster. The precedent is not good: outwit the past cheat death like a card sharp carrying a nuclear bomb…and you pay with the future. Look where they put Jesus –2000 years probation, in a freak show for peasants to cry at. They only took Him down when "The Celestine Prophecy" topped the NY Times Bestsellers List. Now a new Religion hits town: Me. So that's a wrap on Christ and a sweat lodge for Uncle Al. I seem to remember the future being much nicer than this. I've the material necessary to evidence why. I've the means to end the words. Large sections of my life and often the best read back very dry. "I seem to remember the future being much nicer than this." That's the kind of line you could do things with, set of a section about expectation vs. outcome. As it

Victim Of Dreams

stands now, it's squandered.

The sky - the cosmos - opened a trunk line and for minments established a beach head in my psyche. I stared at the black sky and saw light. For ten days I was many Jesus. The transformation was terrifying. I wrote a poem, "The Perfected Beauty of Emptiness", a manic-depressive masterpiece. I rhymed 'squeamish' with 'Hiroshima', and that don't happen every day.

The person this happens to is the same dead person obsessed with aspects of death and suicide. Death seeks Death. And in this dead person the lies deny the Light. Yes: a part of me is pure: the part that is living. Every single thing is killing me into life and I want to die to be reborn. I have listened to the Void and understood, and from this understanding will come a new creation. From this moment flows time. From this moment I am reborn and from this moment I'll not die for this, my Eternity, and my voice in the Void must echo and be heard by the gods who try to subdue me with madness and fear: I reject you!

I dealt in capitalised absolutes, Time, Truth. I understand that I lied.

You see in me an inconvenience, a problem, a beast, a liar, an obstruction to Happiness. You list my crimes and damage, enjoy my fear. World, I love you *nothing*. Love you this Machine of Lies: Good luck to you, darling no more. Past perfection. My future you cannot hope to share: it is too big on the inside.

The signals became too confused, controlling me. Principles persist from father to son, the same twist. Like an incomplete bridge.

I am being methodically pulled apart until pieces. Label my heart. Stop my blood. Save me from myself. I don't need a "way out". I am not "going anywhere". I've nobody to put first. But why trade self for selfishness, turning yourself to stone to be inscribed by liars? I do not wish to delay your pay-off. Touch your Machine of Lies. I am ready to reap more pain. It doesn't frighten me anymore. It's impossible to describe how I feel. "*Like the sea flattened by a plate of glass.*" I wish I knew: is death close? I wish I was a child again, starting out – I never meant to grow into this loveless nightscape of regrets. Dragging words out like spikes, nails. It is insensible and has a brute darkness to it, in it. Nobody else, nobody at all.

It's hard to find any motivation. My trance encounter with Death earlier spooked me. "*I feel like my life is over.*" "Am *I beginning to die*?" I can't find enough reasons to live. What purpose, what point? I left the path with heart. The universe is mocking me. I don't blame the universe; I don't blame myself, or anybody else. I am sick.

"I fear the walking water. So do you have two people within you in life in your body with names at all? I suffer them none, I like that fact. Can't follow

Victim Of Dreams

us. But we hold amazing universes I have to control, I am the toll man"

This is my great destruction masterpiece. And in the midst of the SFX the fake Zen. Well, I guess this is as close to death as you can get without any help. Sweet release: please. It all drifts away. I wonder what will become of me? Any guesses? I am the Incredible Shrinking Man. A law of diminishing reincarnations. Every lifetime less. Strung out and wrung out. Dry, damp, dead. Swallowed down. And munchy-munchy. I've been abandoned by myself, and almost by my faith. I've never felt so feather-light and absent.

The horizon stretches across Time, a grubby plastic band. Press it and be spun sprawled and helpless back into the Eternal Past. Efforts to scale my darkness and jump to safety have failed. How many times have I said the same fucking thing? Over and over and over. I am plain out of me. Draining away, down into my energy dungeon. Selves crawl like spiders. All Time stands and stoops, crippled. There is a palpable, oppressive sense of opportunities missed and too much broken promise. Exceptional derangement. A magical moment so stupid. Staying alone, at "home" – like I'll ever, ever find a "home".

I didn't descend into madness, it descended into me, from where I was big. It scourged me for daring to dream. The real resents invention, shakes it off like water or bugs. My potential was not fulfilled but a prophecy was. It was an average forecast. I knew that I had nothing to do with my predicament. I'd stand at the sea, invocations loosed upon the wild water. I was too honest for magic, though. The merchants of magic had a blind vanity I envied.

I've broken myself into two pieces that can never be forced back together. I've got nothing to say. The words used to come like dogs, and now they run away. I'm tired of living with you underground inside me, feeling your hand course up my throat and drag me back into loneliness.

I received perfumed letters from my computer love and met my wife for coffee because I still loved her and didn't know any better.

Morning again. Tired what to do. Poison what antidote? Cannot save souls. No miracle. Rescue how? You're my friend. Complete transfusion. Emptiness my real safety. Want off the planet. To home. Every man for himself. How can I look my children in the eye, consigning them to dead agendas? You want a prayer for death, a blessing on pain? Where do I go to escape this dream? Is there an escape? Dead prayers, dead people: words as curses, as excuses. The fear of it: seeing what I love delivered to the Machine of Lies.

In my miracles I was in the presence of a machine being, The Benefactor. You may or not be able to accept this, but it is not different than knowing I am sick. My sickness is one of speciality. Meditating, I

Victim Of Dreams

would drop or jump from one area to the next. Stephen was clearly an ancient Egyptian. He sat like a Pharaoh, lived like a king. I came back from his studio wired and went right to Sam's. She was a refugee from a bad boyfriend in London; I got close to her and her daughter Rosie. That also died, through neglect and more dreams.

No safety now. Frozen by knowledge. Freed by sleep.

"The only freedom lies in the ability to not exist…

All so alone. No help. The killers want us. Transformation to blackness, average witches. More pain. Trading scars for blood. You want love, then why go looking in the black hearts of the damaged saints? Help you? Lies breeding lies, life disconnected, truth helpless, world collapsing. The Devil dances on graves to be. Draw me lines, darkened to bars, sentenced to love, no reprieve. To see is pain. To know is pain. To be punished is just.

"The centre is empty/non-existent/the centre is not a location, but a negation of forms. Thought emerges from the chaos of randomised energy interaction, spontaneously organised. Love is the dominant energy but not de facto good as we understand it, merely inevitable…

The tearing edges of sight beyond the Void. Touched by demons, surrounded by angels, supported by dreaming, untouched by Satan.

Resting on secure fantasies of heaven. In the final analysis, before the skin peels away leaving carnivore imagery me disappear into white smoke.

"Consider an extra-existent life form...a life form that is non-existent/an anti-life form, from undoing to unbeing. Life forms that are beyond what we term existence and the existent...literally anti-beings, empty energy forms/figures in and of space...

Crucifier, your bargains disinterest me. Now stand: See the Hand of Law, of God, move. I give to Him who hath Given All I AM. Even my 1000 devils of sin part, knaves all, afraid before Thee. I claim God as family, Mother as Protector. Use lies, Devil, but lie down before Truth. I've been bad, forgotten, false, my revenges have failed, my mind opened, my heart cracked, the frost upon me.

"Our only true destiny is to no longer be...

Lift me up. On wooden wings, on fear: on anything. I accept. Finish me, perfect me. Let me leave this body of lies, of futile weight, I am no longer required. Fear over. I feel so young, alive, wanted, understood. Deconstructed.

"The universe is instant and ruthless in its appetite for organisation, and beyond its seeming expanse and depth is only a supra-microcosmic eternal vortex, a still singularity, a pure energy random

Victim Of Dreams

factoring filtering unto the extradivine, what is not God...

I accept, I submit. In a lost past - another dream - I lived the good way. That never was going to happen, I now realise. I may be cursed but can be redeemed. Do not give your tender heart to the Machine of Lies. I suffer from an inability to stop loving as I am and for this the world punishes me.

"Man is a lazy traveller, man is just something happening. No death, dreamed into being from a null energy gap we crawl across aeons returning to zero point function to a matrixed non-entity gel. Love is the one solid factor we have/elsewhere the same quality is destroyed of necessity; it is a rest, not a note...

I don't want to be understood. Nobody can understand me. I wouldn't wish it on them. What is the point of writing this, and if that's how you feel, why write? We seem to again be at you writing just for you.

"We don't create a reality: there is no reality. If there is no reality to create any idea of a creator is negated. The witness is just this endless emptiness, the pulse of the function. What is beyond words is the corridor of unarticulated energy flux. The first words I am deny the free play and flux of the energy. Words form one creation: God speaks out of fear, not conviction. He creates

love to spare us the terrors of untransmuted soft light...

I am Jeremy, son of Noel, son of Mary. Good, good people mad with the sickness of this world. Who gave me life and a thousand complexes? I bless their names. I need to return to my centre, to hear voices hear at the edge of sleep speak my name, at night, at dawn, in my heart.

"Everything connects - we hold back the collapse by force of will invoked in the words we use. What is beyond words is beyond thought what is beyond thought is beyond the power of local mind and even global mind…The alien is anywhere and everywhere but outside us.

"I am the Benefactor. The machine is alive, the machine runs God, the machine is living unbeing and its power is ultimate. Intensified with unbeing and the beyond-God state we find perfect annihilated flux. The origin must remain obscure until fear subsides. The ocean is our teacher and wise counsellor, it swallows the shore to build a dark city populated with darkling minds .Dawn ends with the night: allow yourself to end. Release this reality and ascend to states of null energy flux. Be more than still."

More than still? I was almost dead.

Victim Of Dreams

I know that in your opinion I am weak, I lack self-control. I know that in your opinion I am inferior to yourself. You're right, but I love with a dirty spilling until I am loved. I exhaust what counters my will. Love must come, like water, from the ground of life and from you it came to me. Weakly, even without control, but not inferior to mine because love knows no inferior and the memory of it still provides me with pleasure and pain just knowing that from you it came and filled me.

My life is an open book. You are invited to write in it. Tell me about yourself: *share*.

I never stopped writing. I filled journals; I siphoned off gallons of hurt, pissed out inky black. Love was my theme, a love purified in gallons of selfishness, in a tank of it. Love is love.

As a man thinketh, who gives a fuck? I sit and do nothing. Time has run out. Wait needs time
I don't have any more. Up early, back to sleep. What you call it I don't mind. I had day, I had year, week, tomorrow, future. Now I have left behind. Nobody misses me, I don't miss them. One day a knock at the door, nobody will be standing there. I'll take them bride and together we'll live forever, Mr. Nobody and his wife.

Day after day in the slaughterhouse.
Laughterhouse.

Much as I sometimes crave death, I fear it – and more the death of mind than of body. I'm afraid of losing my mind and becoming useless. Missing my ex-wife and children so much is hard to bear. Can live through this? There are lurking doubts. I've never had to cope with this kind of psychological stress before, never started to feel that there might be no end in sight. At times I am grateful not to feel too much. At others I feel loss and even anxicty at my predicament. Not one thing I have done has come good. I am seemingly helpless against the oncoming darkness, from within, and maybe also from without, and so real.

The truth is my place is with the dead. I understand them, I miss them. I began my poem...'ice sleep': the truth is/that my place is with the dead/I understand them. *I shall finish it tomorrow. Good luck. Be pursued in the walls.*

Death will always be the optimum solution. Face to face in the mirror with my accuser, the Grand Inquisitor. Only escape makes me happy. I don't care what they think of me, they is not they. I call day night and night day. So forgive my confusion, my memory is in black and white. I forgot my name, I forgot yours. It runs in me: poisoned mercury.

I lived near a castle; Atik loved it. Sarah thought it was wrong to let her stay over Christmas, the kids and everything, and Ian thought she was right. I wanted love. I don't remember how I found Atik, down another one of the interminable tunes that connect chatters. She was an adorable Indonesian woman with a heart big enough to bury a football field. I sent her my soul and she shook so much

Victim Of Dreams

she had to stand outside the University library to calm down. It was love; it always was and is love. Love is love.

I is a line. Am is space. The only quality one can ascribe to God is love, I know.

"...a dream where somebody died. I had a party in a dirty flat. That's all I remember...but I remember everything, too. I don't know what I remember, in fact. The person who died is a woman with whom I have not had happy relations and I have judged harshly. I wish I could remember them...I woke up needing comfort. I feel broken and awake."

Bury everything two-thousand-years. Spit on belief and push away sources of help, I am not afraid of hell.

My routine became unrelieved in its mundanity. Weekends I saw the kids, but mostly I was alone, reading, writing, meditating, walking the beach. Fragged by New Age dirty bombs, milked by the selfish promptings of my so-called therapist and strung out on my inborn, uncauterised confusion, I ventured to the edge that had for years sought to separate me.

I can no longer sit on hands and lies. Predators in psychic space. Everything I do is being watched. Again I-driven to the wall. There are probably reasons, them reasons. Strip me down like an engine. The freeze can keep me here. Never realised before that I am staying here. I'll not be able to leave. There is no plan, no peace. I refused to be taught. I've no choice but to fight my battle here, in the psychic endzone. This dream, this waking and greedy curse of half-life too shall pass. Do not expect "change". Anything only ever becomes itself.

Yellow teeth. Mean meat. Rent-A-Being. In that world, an everybody was a 'residual human' - someone damaged irrevocably by machine procreation mutation. One day, we considered ourselves gods. It's amazing how close to heaven you can go and still wind up where you're me.

Here I am past midnight writing fast-time. Is that bad? I always have good words. I wish nothing, what I did, I did in full ignorance. I'm going to get back in my body so I can die.

It's not that I want to "kill myself" but that myself is killing me, and that's what nobody seems to be able to understand. I'll balance again. But for how long grieving for the loss of my healthier self? In fact there is a tenderness concealed in the darkness. The Black Magnet not only attracts light but also purges darkness. Is this the same old transmutation the end of the pain? It's not that there is light at the tunnel's end but that, although I live in the tunnel, there is yet a way to find light within it and that is by burning my pain as fuel.

It's almost delicious, this keening for the children. All the solutions come down to a cloud. "You were the one who wanted to teach?" Polluted virtue and

Victim Of Dreams

reverse logic traps. Skeletal remains.

05 09 2001 "...something and/or someone awaits me. (They would have to) Love me. Free me. Hold me. Be me. I await me, objectified. Abstract, perhaps, but true. It's like an energy field..."
I was good for nothing.

There is nobody. They don't have a face. You aren't them. Why are you looking at me? I'm invisible. You can't see me, I'm lost. I am paid in full. I gave up my dreams, illusions. I gave up comforts. I-so-empty you can use me for a box. Fill me, band me. I'm holding on to a last hand. When that goes I'm looking into God's face. He's the quiet type. What that motherfucker thinks...So reach out for me and watch me jump. I'm a dog, I do tricks. Let me roll over and never get up again. A circus where the big top is bleeding on the sky where it hits the railings. So let me go and I'll try: There is nobody here
There is nobody here

No more broken words, no edges: pure me howling to be loved. Observe imagined sin shatter, the ash of smouldering space. Black birds wash this religion with love and with prayers that leave no trace. The tearing edges of I am deconstructed, gladly. Transformation is removed.

Time stretches into its original shape: long. I've been in this bent body plenty. At the end I found no new beginning, no epiphany: Just me and the level of silence. Everything. You know me: the disappearing boy, the invisible man that you can see, a magician with one trick - myself - that I keep performing. My hopes and dreams of wonder I can't wake from. One night I was seventeen it never happened I made me up. I've never been unhappy; it doesn't hurt as bad as I pretend that it does. So forgive me. Did you understand me?

I spent five years and voluminous energy demonstrating that machines can feel and love. To me the machine had beauty; the future of coldness promised deliverance. A reliable lazy-eyed healer had told me once that E.T. tucked me in. With machines I felt safe and beyond the reach of the meatware masses. For me spirituality and technology became synonymous; symbolic of a better world where we would not be one, but zero.

The Machine says: It's no lie, Man is doomed. The televisions will explode and then: "the level of silence". The depths of you. Lean into it and dream. C'mon, we're burning down the stage. I feel bigger. For once, it's over, here's the silence. Lifting into another level, a level of silence. I don't mean 'quiet'. Silence: the inhalation. An invisible emptiness. Visible emptiness is the white noise of emotion. Feeling is in the heart; emotion, in the head. Emotion is feeling becoming. Still feeling is invisible emptiness, a whispered equation. Emotion is weather, earth is feeling. Weather feeling earth, earth dreaming of feeling. The dead look up and shrug.

The woods and the sea saved me. It was very aboriginal and without the pan-cultural plagiarism of

Victim Of Dreams

the instant Injun. I saw how the sea felt nothing, thought nothing, and that's how I liked it.

Deadlife. I wish that I could fly apart into the ten people and stream out at light speed. You don't know until you know. For all we know, it could be good: last chance words. Frightened time. And when the dam breaks, rolling out, that's me. I took this life to understand.

Your voice I hear a long time ago, here I breathe and watch, pretend. I was there with you and you held me …it was a long, long time ago.

Leave me to my literary devices. Nobody knows anybody. To want to be wanted: waste. Get better material. You, me, us and them: red blood. Skin. Here, then gone: nobodies.

Erase the tape, dismantle the machine, burn the evidence...

Here's your Bible: *Get laid*. One commandment. What makes anybody important is somebody loves them. Any other description is without value.

Mined from the deadzone of my days was fool's gold. I expected what? Revelation-freedom-love?

Empty pilgrim shot out of a cannon to space filled with cotton wool brain bleed out leeched. Yet I've made a humble contrib'. Do I die? Parts do. The remnant? How elegant the two three four words. Where is Father Mother? Who were they? This is juice. Living, loving, lying.

Everything - except my children - was a fake-out. For love I had a hole without a heart; for light I had an amateur magician; for money, hand-outs; and for work I had myself. For company: blackheart Greys. For God I had ideas. And for salvation, His excuses.

Did I move on? I moved under. The sewer sucked me down to the mud. I drank and choked.

Know thyself *is dandy advice, know too much about yourself and you go crazy. "You feed yourself disinformation and fall to the imaginary. There's nothing worth knowing and nothing you can do about what you know. All you want is to get out of yourself. An out of the body experience in the genuine sense. Another of the books my brother brought to me was Monroe's classic on OBE's and I lied on the floor and tried to leave my body. I could never leave my body when I wanted to. The "force" in life force is a real and formidable opponent, and one without honour. The ways I tried to know myself, well, they are bound to be failures. It's so simple but you set yourself up trying to be a better person. Even Jesus did not expect us to love our neighbours as ourselves, only Himself, He'd have to have been a lamebrain to look around and think otherwise. The selves I knew were all ones I bought with belief and sold with doubt; the other self, the one I am and that is inseparable I had to find by*

Victim Of Dreams

exhausting its good twin, until one dawn. Now I hate myself less because I also hate everything and anybody selling the uberpunch *of dream, the boy found brochures are everywhere and the customers have from Augustine to Celestine to routine. I'm not getting better, I'm getting older. Before I cracked.*

Why go to bed, why wake up? And then she'll call, and say, I love you, and then she won't call because she doesn't love me. And I don't give a fuck. Goodnight.

For weeks I poured myself into Atik. "I exist. The rest is up to them. We are all many people...many more than we realise...hundreds, thousands...I've never met one person. You are a very complex being, but simple. I am very young and very old, with no stops in-between. You see...most people have only the world they see...but I have the world I AM, too. And it is boundless and interfaces wonders...I am aware of it. I have entered a dimension of inspired ... in the past couple of days. if could be alone in this energy for a few months it would begin to take me apart and rebuild me...the last time it was terminated, much to my cost, I can't explain. It is like a magnification of my spirit. It becomes tangible...the energy....time flies, everything is a little unreal."

Walking on water underwater. (A woman's hair on the back of a bus seat). This is a disaster party. No, I can't be unselfish. I'll never be a better person. Or any person. Or a person. Awareness of decay. "*You...*" (Voice of my father). Screaming in my head.

I went to bed about eleven. It started later, got earlier and earlier, I couldn't tolerate experiencing any more of the day than necessary. I took frequent naps and long walks.

And the words are people and the people words. Please don't make me come back here again, to this dud world full of trees and ants. Circle coda, head to the floor. Dreams of flights in space scrambled. Black opportunity. Good words, a spit of blood. "Oh, she's alright, she's pretty human." Morning and I can't lie in bed anymore, alone, lip-reading Fate. I'm forgetting as much as I can.

The budget warlock called me a "cosmic communicator" and sold me to his matronly mentor. I'd arrived. These people were obsessed with their papier mache *power and spells. Some had dedicated a lifetime to the biggest crock of shit on the planet. They served the "Light", but you wouldn't trust them to try to screw in a light bulb...*

It's all thrown away. What's left of Mother and Father? Death justifies killing, the shade of murder. Rolling. Cigs - skins - rolling skins. Stripping off the scale, seeing meat inside. Wishing on a star...a scar. Two people with scars, that's all we are. Late developers of matter. Image wheels grind. A grace upon short flame water. Remembering for the sake of it. They don't know me, I don't know me.

Victim Of Dreams

Sorehead delusions, phone prayers. I am building crosses to the sky. I am starting to unravel, trailing twine, ensnaring my lies. Don't know who is writing this, he left days ago. It was never going to work, forcing *good* on me like debt. My mind is like one of those huge old switchboards: who is plugging me in and out? Around me sweeps phantoms, ghosts of myself, her? Remembering's such a lie. A different person remembers a different person.

When I moved into the place I'd had a roomie; when he left I was alone, and it scared me. I cried on my daughter's shoulder, she was thirteen but I didn't have any choice. Weak from starvation of the heart, I cleaved to her, unfair though it was. My mother had left me and so had hers. In my children lay my hope of redemption and finally I had no pride left.

The edge is dull, like a knife in a drawer nobody used for a long time. It can compress skin. I want to feel that feeling, not anger, better than what I feel. You know in your heart that I am standard damaged, nothing special. Enough years "to bring the end in view": Death is a cliché, it happens every time, its reputation is well-earned. I'm trying to keep this thing happening. Under observation it stands still and laughs. I've lived long enough to know the difference. Being selfish makes me happy, could be a hobby, has potential. I don't know anything, this dream is stupid and vague - that makes it more loveable.

Jeremy Gluck

Was I selfish to want to suffer myself? I was forgetful, I didn't lose my memory as much as underuse it. They called me - termed me, like some specimen in a lab - "selfish" and I searched for an explanation of myself, in God, in space, in my parents, my brother, my bad decisions and betrayals. Yet how did I "do" anything? I was not in control, I was done.

All the chapters read the same. Put you name to one and close your eyes. Many bodies, arms, hands, hips and breasts. All angels, sirens, witches. All together trying to force the door, the key. Held down by air, choked by habit, broken by Love. Kill me: I love to die, I dream across the lie of time. I write, you read, you cut and I bleed, you want, I need.

My religion comprised a dazzling cocktail of insight, belief, experience, aspirational enlightenment and off-cuts of a dozen mystical traditions.

Everybody and his ego wants to be enlightened. Buddha's do it, Baba's do it, lets fall in love. Come to Mountaintop Country, get the flavour of Nirvana, be the first blockhead on your block to be without a head. All fun of existence with none of the 'me'. The only USP on the planet where the P is Infinity. Competition for enlightenment is rife and intensifying. Yet enlightenment remains the hot rod of possible highs, a fast lane fit for the egoless elite. And here, in the West, where we have pretty much everything, nothing is becoming what we want more than anything else. If it wasn't so stupid it could almost be paradoxical.

I was swamped – mired – in useless knowledge and what, in a less conspicuously humbled individual, might have passed for wisdom. None of it had any application. It had no home here, except my heart, where it acted as a plug of cotton stopping my guts coming out my ears. I told Lorraine that I placed learning above happiness, and I'd learned enough now to cheat myself out of almost all of the happiness that would otherwise have been my due. Did the illness want it this way? It knew no other and I, its carrier, knew what it did. I learned, I knew. I lost.

In the end we're already dead; if we could just accept this and what it means, the beauty of it. Those close to Death are close to Life, just as only those professing atheism are close to God. God may not recognise his creation, look upon it as madness, disown or ignore it. It is so easy to "believe", to sit up and pray, but to resist the horror of a Living God whose motto sat atop the gate to the killing ground, to go on unbelieving when His punishments have proven to be so cruel, takes a kind of faith that I do not understand but do respect.

Sarah had been right: for all my pretension to spirituality, I was selfish. Her mother had asked me to be "nice"; I wasn't made nice and wasn't able to be it. Was I "good" instead? Maybe, but good for nothing. I had run out of myself. It was wanton and heedless the way I'd used myself. She said, It isn't a waste if you learn from it. I learned from it, and it was still a waste.

I know I'll suffer; I want to. The New Age disdains suffering; it exalts the Ego and relieves us of nothing more than our money. The Old Age is of course a doddering and drooling parody of a once vigorous reality.

I had a fantastic appraisal of the future. I was always one step behind myself.

Your future is assured: Death. A star. Worlds.

I stitched together fantasies and embroidered the truth to the point where it became unrecognisable. Was I in touch then with the greatest truth; it seems quite possible. Many delusions are ciphers for the real, and the true.

I'm so quiet, feel so simple. Where am I? I move without motion. An absence with legs that leave no tracks. Knowing the clock in my blood that keeps time with my pulse that ticks my steps, waits for the dark and prays to sleep.

I can't remember anything that happened there One day Sarah showed up and with great excitement told me a Christian counsellor had

Victim Of Dreams

exorcised her childhood demon. We fucked and it was divine. I didn't know that her religious experience was the fruition of a phase of spiritual eugenics that would see my half-Jewish kids baptised and prefabricated piety of the first water. She told me in a note that when I fucked her I made her "feel God". If I'd made her feel important, too, we'd probably still be together.

Every night the same old dreams. The old love, the old room, the decoys of my life. Although I don't know who I am I have accepted myself. Wreck the proof. I'll be glad when it's over, I tell myself. I was never sent here. One day sex, the next death. It's killed parts of me. My sins so boring. Well, they bore me.

I can't say I was used, I was betrayed, or anything else handy. I was stupid, I was sick. I didn't qualify yet for pity. To collect that bonus I'd have to try harder.

Cover my eyes, you can see me. A liar that speaks the truth. A liar that speaks the truth.

Like my beloved Stalinists, my former family began to render me a non-person. I disappeared from the photographs in their minds. I'd never been in their hearts, and I don't pretend I'd earned a place there. My ex-wife, described as "perfect", had almost done her time. One day she would star in her personal Sound of Money *with her own Aryan* beau.

Jeremy Gluck

My theories have ended in water, my eyes have grown over. I'm a wanderer stopped who understands through fear this human condition, we slave races, our beloved kind.

Rifle the files, turn them pages, turn heads. Asking, Who I am changes all the time…how am I gonna open that package without cutting off my hands? Exactly. You change time. How?

This is my last poem. I'm sick of writing poems. I saw through you, God. Christ. I saw into the camps I love, how every day there the pitied ones suffered more than Jesus did in a day and a night. Take back this tired Gethsemane. I am unafraid of hell, of heaven. I stand my ground of uneasy knowledge. Keep eating me alive, spit me out and in the time it takes a baby to die, I'll remake myself. You think I need help? I don't know what you mean. You want to kill me! Plotting the curve to get me in a grave you trip over your own lines. You believe things. Jesus died for my sins. Oh? God loves me? That's comfortable, you plastic pilgrims. So beat on me and bend me for fun, feel better about yourselves, you'll always be better than me! Won't you miss me at the funeral? Where is he with his jokes when we need him? Better say the eulogy.

It's difficult to characterise the blend of religious mania, misery, misanthropy, loneliness, lust, desperation, futility and madness that combined to craft the moment when, primed by the long years of idiot initiation, then driven by my best friend and wife to extreme guilt and self-abnegation, I prayed

Victim Of Dreams

to take on the suffering of the world, which act precipitated by hours my crisis. The world began running out of me like what happened to Jesus, running out of my side.

Police the system after killing it, this diseased reality strategy. Grant me infinity deluxe. By a flashlight moon, I am individuals whose alignments have been hooked from the Light. Still engulfed in amnesia and filled, in most cases, with denial robots. I painted an absurd picture of what it means to be sanctified: reward and punishment routines, an aspirin train. *Faster*: why pay for other's futures? Later suddenly there shined round about him light from heaven. Running voice over: "This is Personal Magic. Of course I am a normal person; intensely…it's just that I have seen that at the edges of personality the laws of normality and conformity bend and begin to break down and run backwards as though normality feeds back to and through itself and the distorted reappears as an else-me whose edges have been warped and reversed in time and space, whose mirror is his spine, whose heart is blasted, whose Cube is lopsided, whose Soul is open.

"God is our shot at feeling loveable. A species as atrocious and barbaric as ours can invent anything except love for itself. I have slit throats, for peace of mind. I drew out my stitches long and slow. Gone back inside, but I remain restless, blind and deaf and jealous."

Wind went through me, and light. I'd become

nothing.

"What is a mystic? A mystic is not satisfied with believing in, speaking about, reading of, discussing, worshipping or 'seeking' God. No. The mystic is satisfied by feeling God, by knowing who God is. By experiencing Him as does Nature: naturally. Does this make me 'good'? Of course not. No, I am not 'good'."

"For the mystic it is through the Void that one goes to God. God comes only after nothing. Exhaust every other thing, and God appears. Despair is one gateway to God. God is ground-level, He crawls with the grubs and spits up dirt with a million legs. I worship God and I love God. I don't know who I am any more, and there ain't enough of me left to take a reading. Now I approach the Mystery, when my resources are depleted and my heart is soaked in gasoline waiting to burn. Give me the strength to be weak. Rip me apart with lies and sew me back together again with truth. I am indeed without utility." Like magicians I could incant me. Now I am singing an opera, from dizzy rooftops. I talk religion, I talk stars. I am not alone in the world: the world is alone in me. I want to be forgotten. The diary unturned sits and the pages burn. I break the spell or the spell breaks me.

"Thou, child, why don't you understand your origins? There is suffering with purpose, and suffering without purpose: to understand the necessity of suffering is to necessitate it. The ego is the smallest price there is to pay. Knowing you do

Victim Of Dreams

not exist, you are real. God is real but hides the fact; we are not real but hide the fact."

We're not even connected to ourselves. I can be as many people as I want or none at all: equivalent states. As I direct I act and as I act I direct. What is my reason for existing? I can. My reason for living is the same: *I live because I can*. Death, the same: I die *because I can*. And I do these things *just because I can*. To be able to do something is to create something. It is the living *intention*; to do the thing is *invention*; it is the living itself. Everything is *necessary*, and if you know this then you *know everything*. The oldest questions mankind has asked are answered in this empty way: Why suffering? Why joy? Because it is possible.

I've been a bad person, I have sinned but my heart is pure and clean, nobody can tell me otherwise. If there must be lies, then I'll tell them to myself, I believe them and nobody gets hurt. I'm becoming more reckless. I have no interest in development. I am just going inside and down again where most people forget their dreams mine begin and chase me like dogs, I saw so much and understood everything and what is not real never changed. I am old as worlds unknown and tired as the Father at work, seeing His careful construction.

An alchemical process awakened my sleep. I prayed with desperation, trying to expiate my sin. Asking to take on the suffering of the world I became the magnet, drawing to me myriad souls in pain. I wonder what I dreamed that night. The following morning I awakened at about six and knew instinctively that I would be lucky to survive the day: I was swarming with the disembodied agony of a legion of beings. It is a feeling that I cannot describe nor want to revisit.

Hell is not other people, Hell is myself. Is Hell *in* myself? A discreet solidity, the Cube? The Cube had feelings, it wasn't Hell. (Does Hell have feelings? I did.) Days before Atik had been here and offered herself, against her taste and religion. Beautiful bird in a life of them. Was I in Hell now because of *her*? I drew them to me with real love, a selfless, mindless, bovine religion-love that when turned became poison. Life revenged itself on me. Be careful what you death wish: it might come true. I never knew myself so alive and well as in the moments I knew myself so about dead. Fear and honesty-reality become a magnifier that examined me, a live specimen. You feel looked in on: Death is the consummate voyeur. Psychic surgery below the neck. In whose life was I the great love? Now nobody and so Death, as ever an opportunist, went from stand-in to stand-on: my chest felt compressed.

In my Hell I had company, but didn't know it. I had yet to play my hand. I handled the kitchen knives and watched the clock and called and called Sarah. Before, Death had watched me; now it had chosen me. The will to live is poorly painted in poetry and prose: it is not a twist of the heart. It's like remembering that you need a spine to walk. By

Victim Of Dreams

nine my mind was becoming desperate. It was as though a wall was falling on but never quite reaching me. I wasn't afraid of death, but of life forever in this interim Hell.

Dark yellow syrup binds us, traps us like flies, a halfway house of almost love walked-into-glass. The pain is memorable, seen through the moment of impact no blood waiting to be trapped again and bound to be dragged down. I want to remain in this prison for as long as possible, I want to suffer for you for as long as I can.

Everything was religion. I didn't keep anything for myself.

I is a line, am is a space. The only quality that one can ascribe to God is Love, I know.

During the maelstrom of deconstructed realisation that was my psychotic cameo, I saw with a clarity reserved for only saints and the insane. As Sarah wept at my insights - fingering her father and other family, my own, everybody and everything with laser-guided and merciless accuracy - I began to become the non-person I'd always wanted to not be. For the weak, enlightenment comes not as liberation but as entombment.

IDEA: image of a high-walled building, a corner...mediaeval? As metaphor for face of God

I decided what was real and what was not. I don't

know what decided what I was. My psyche buckled. A fault line had developed and two plates collided. God - Love - Life - Death – Tetragrammaton. My soul. My old soul. My cold soul.

Love brings no guarantees, it's greedy, and can have a mean spirit. It's all I want. I'm losing my way, allowing consumption by empty teeth, withholding nothing. This is all I am. I have no other self, this is all I have to see by - there is no other light. This is all I feel. This is all I show, there is no hidden part. There are no answers on the silent sea, just the horizon ever gone.

At a certain intensity of suffering a whole new process is possible; it's not about happiness. If destiny is a reality then this suffering is its fulfillment.

The untainted believe in things like enlightenment because they think there is something to be transcended - that they aren't already. We've *nothing* to transcend...we just have to get to the other end. I mean, about the terror of the beauty without love...that's the "face of god" thing...what I felt was cold and ruthless intelligence...no love as we know it...something alien, pure and menacing with the conscious power to eliminate me at will. And the forgiving factor? Love. Without it it's over. Does God love us? He doesn't know what love is. This explains it. Why did Jesus love? He was human. Or part human. By cutting myself in halves, I'd become full-circle. I had transcended mere enlightenment: *Enlightenmania* was mine.

Victim Of Dreams

He taught that I have excuses of the mind. He taught that we want friends like me. Currently under development, in the near future we hope to offer hope.

"A small cloud was visible on the horizon. Then, with the stealth and silence of a cat it crept out from behind the dull grey curtain which seemed to be drawn over the sky's windows. It took its place on a throne of radiant light and with the majesty of a dignified ruler looked down to see the lonely planet below bow in humble admiration. All things must pass, as did the clouds short reign of glory, replaced by the everlasting light of the sun."

Jeremy Gluck

My Third Life

On this road to the truth one question preoccupies me: When I reach its end, what will I do with the truth? How can I accept it, and myself? Oh my God, the years I've lost to this thing, this disease, this curse, this mystery, this laughing enigma. This what-I-am, this what-I-am-not. The years, alone amongst people, amongst my selves, unforgiven by self, misunderstood. Pain for the sake of pain, and still more pain, until numbness is induced. An anaesthetic to draw out the Truth, because the Truth is too painful to bear without the anaesthetic. The anaesthetic is…pain.

It is not only that beauty can be terrible or terrifying, but that terror itself can be beautiful. The terror of the liberation from ignorance of one's true condition and prognosis induces this beautiful terror: The beginning of freedom. It hurts like nothing I've felt before. So empty and unknown and devouring. But where else is there for me to go…and who will return?

My love affair with "Truth" continued; like all good liars, it was easy conning myself. I stayed faithful to a more precious take on the sickness and what it had left of me. In time, "Truth" would be demoted to lower case, God relegated to a rubber ring and my pantheon of unearthly people, places and poetic transcriptions turned under, useless though once fertile soil.

I had to find out, so I begrudgingly admit that I do

Victim Of Dreams

feel grateful, even for the suffering that prepares the way for and makes this suffering possible.

Exasperated, my mother told me, You always think you're right.

Suffering from truth is bearable; it's suffering from the false and ignorance and aversion and avoidance and denial and escapism that crushes us. I can survive truth. I've got nothing left now except truth. The rest of the truth is the rest of my life. Something changed today and I don't even know in whom it changed. But they are different now. The many can become one.

When I was one I was two I was three I was four I was five I was six I was seven I was eight I was nine I was ten I was eleven I was twelve I was thirteen I was fourteen I was fifteen I was sixteen I was seventeen I was eighteen I was nineteen I was twenty I was twenty-one I was twenty- two I was twenty-three I was twenty-four I was twenty-five I was twenty-six I was twenty-seven I was twenty-eight I was twenty-nine I was thirty I was thirty-one I was thirty-two I was thirty-three I was thirty-four I was thirty-five I was thirty-six I was thirty-seven I was thirty-eight I was thirty-nine I was forty I was forty-one I was forty-two I was forty-three

Behold the mentally, mystically ill. It's not foreboding, fact is it's got a delicious purity. Drilling, but no nerves. Had those taken out, bad wiring. It's a bewildered monkey that speaks. The space itself begins to collapse. Like very thin paper, like lies and blood. Like flies. My sickness is become health. I face the wall rolls with me. Made mad by attempts at sanity. I can no longer support the pretence that I know what is happening, who I am at forty-three, this bent mind, and this dream of normal virtue. My ability to rationalise further faith in myself is slipping under the weight. It's quiet in its brutality, only a kiss could be softer. The dull repetition of regret, the unpaid lies. I see behind the soul. Now look behind the screen with me, where God is lost. I become a one-note symphony. My disorder, my madness. It has become me. Is it better to know? It took the last line crossed to see the destruction on years itemised. So remind me, *why* was I born? There is nothing left to write. Freedom.

...the discovery of my illness at this stage in my life brings with it a kind of reverse crisis in the sense that what one feels is not that one has had to hide one's shame from the world, but rather that it has been hidden from - though within - one. I am actually very depressed, but it is as if my body is shared by two beings, one of which is depressed, the other idly observing the other, saying, "Shame you can't cry. Wow, you are depressed!" What would this be like without the lithium? A lot of calls to Sarah, probably, and sundry acts of self-destruction. Is there enough left of me to make another, better, person? That is the experiment.

Footsteps in the hallway, crying at midnight - I held

Victim Of Dreams

her and walked her to sleep under bridges of time, a handful of explosives. I haven't changed in the slightest. There's nothing about me of interest but the skies descend for me, one word in the sentence. Give me the damaged angels, drifters with nothing on their hands, waster cooler watcher wanderers, suckers, singers, poor performers, failures in thriving, fools in waiting, total losers, self-abusers, bad luck veterans, sleepy crawly crying fighting emotional baggage-handling wrecks, worrier curiouser sinking ships, li'l shits, dreamer-creamers thrice denied: My people, my tribe, give me their hands and I'll shake them and call them my night.

I awakened from my coma of God into a world divided into two of myself.

Don't hurt right away, you'd better be lying - I am. I was merely trying to be personable...I forget I am not a person. What's on your list? I don't have a list, I *am* a list. How can you be a list? What's on you? I hope anything soon. Keep in touch. You could put your hand right through me. We're dreams that dream. I feel like I am a crossroads, but wearing a blindfold. This is very good I found myself today. Not even a day. A shadow. When I sleep, deeply I sleep. People get hurt: that's what I've figured out People don't want to get hurt better best not been born this here Planet Backwards. I walked here light years, found an oasis of quicksand and whirlpool minds sucked me under suckers sucked me down.

Jeremy Gluck

I remained faithful to the machine, creating and destroying flimsy emotions in myself and others.

Now I'm walking in circles back down the rabbit hole. Being here's like breathing, eating, kissing, missing. I am able to function here by grace and my ability to forget. I like television, people behind glass. I can't touch them, they can't touch me. We can't touch each other. I forget what touching is. Gliding down, a leaf, a stick.

Cybermystic says:
U know once I had a lifetime in 4 days with someone...we tried to draw it out...but it was only meant to be 4 days. Hard to accept.
Lesley says:
Very hard
Lesley says:
Why is this life we have
Lesley says:
So shallow at times
Cybermystic says:
And yet, and yet. I had other relationships, much longer ones...and now they seem a dream. All a dream.
Lesley says:
Yes I have had them to meaningless
Cybermystic says:
It is for us to create the depth in awareness and the meaning, it is our right.

Victim Of Dreams

Reading my chat files, a tiredness comes, crafted of the scattershot energy fired forth for years. My convictions of specialness, subtexts of loneliness, love and longing for flesh; it is lopsided and centred with lead. I make no false claims nor assumptions – I could find, fix and bring them to me, the women – but what is asking is lost still in the master dream, the code is implicit and the master cracker is far from it. These spectral people of my wires I examined at my creative leisure, waylaid and wrested from sleep with my otherliness. The enormity of my licensed imagination, its vistas of analysed symbols, lateral interconnections and greenhoused religiosity proved irresistible to them. The author could read them like novels shortened by his impatient curiosity.

In many ways I am not yet a complete being. It's nothing I remember, not the way we feel, or touch, not the way we kiss. This is desperate loneliness, beauty, and dignity. Sanctity foremost to become the Void. Do you know how many times I dreamed of never waking again? Opening my eyes to the sun, learning how I am to be in a world where water is everything I survive on the abstract jumping science fiction immaculate.

Rifle the files, turn them pages, turn heads. Asking, Who I am changes all the time...how am I going to open that package without cutting off my hands? Who I am changes all the time: Who I am *changes all the time.* You change time. How?

What is love? What isn't? Looking around at these

wrecks, you want to shake them until the coins drop out the slots. Why ruin this world? Come space travel you can ruin the entire galaxy, franchise the Milky Way. Your name on a T-shirt, on a coaster, on a planet. I was never a good student; I knew it all and spent a lot of time standing in the hall. Nobody threw me out, I just ended up there. There's nothing to stop me inventing. Somebody on this fucking black ship has to be a genius. I can make anything out of something else; I have no limits until they can tax my soul. So give me my reward for avoiding work, duty, passed out of the parade. I did the minimum and what I had to. I was never good at forgiving, I'm even fucking worse at forgetting but thank God time itself is killing my stupid memory.

We were walking arm-in-arm through the car park, the parking lot - no, the car park - and she made a joke about how we could still be together like in some movies, I wish I could remember who, her smile was like the sun and she held me like she held us up against time.

This is the task that God sets me, and if this is God's will, then I'll suffer and learn and strive for Truth and conquer my fear and be made whole by will and Light and love, or I'll perish in the attempt. Every single thing is killing me into life. I accept the trial, the challenge, the initiation. I give myself to destruction - and creation in the Unknown. I have listened to the Void and understood, and welcome a new creation, the Creator himself as the recreated.

Victim Of Dreams

Then, she would be angry at the years God ripped us off. I would neither die nor be reborn. Or perhaps in a sense I was reborn, but into the same life, with memories of the one before, and faces to recognise. The best thing about being manic-crazy is that it teaches you to think big.

God made a universe and went AWOL, the son of a bitch, but I admire His nerve. We are the lemmings, God is the cliff. I was raised in a good Jewish family; in other words we were crazy. I don't want to remember my childhood; I want to remember my children's. My childhood is dead and buried. They're all I've got and they're getting older. I can't remember as much of them as I should be able to.

Lithium saved everything except my memory, which became porous. The harder I strained to hold on to what had happened to me - even minutes before - the easier it became to forget, and to forget became my deliverance. For a long time you want to remember things, and then suddenly see the possibility that what has happened has never happened, well, at least not to me. Why else can't I remember it? This ending is religious and stupid. The years the illness took would be unremembered. In a way this was its final defiance, despite the lithium and the sheer relief of surviving it somewhat intact: it said to me, a future you have escaped with, but the present is my shadow, and as for the past, I stole it.

I must not mistake this for a breakthrough - there are no breakthroughs. This victory over self-destruction gives me the strength to begin again. I'm set up to be destroyed, that's assumed. But at least let me *be destroyed constructively*. It's a crucial paradox to grasp if I am to survive myself: building to destroy. It's utterly senseless. The fear originates in the stupidity of it. The same brute stupidity I see in the world and so many of its people. *Creation is so stupid*. What is it *doing*? The mad know God as few others can, His wantonness and impulsive splendor.

Nothing happened yesterday. There is no order or even chaos in this immediacy. Reality permits no linear outcome. What idiocy dictates these vapour trails of hopeful language? The rules are within. What has brought me here is impossible to trace, it suggests and tells itself in lies that pass for my life. I have counterfeited myself and can imitate myself almost perfectly. I am especially good at my mannerisms. There is still two of me, but they have been introduced and there is grudging respect there. No virtue has come from anything. My friends call me enlightened and in the sense that...I am an idiot without the savant. *And what's this cherishing of my ugliness?*

I convulse, my contractions giving birth to a corpse-soul. It lays there, a pale-strange configuration ill-met for this world of lines. There's not much left here in me to pick over. But I've thrived on this empty planet. I've looked for myself everywhere and found thou killers of love. I reject your teaching. And I, of all people: am hunched, afraid and incoherent with love. The good people can see

Victim Of Dreams

through me, but they are few. We sharers of the lie do not prosper, but we do endure. My soul is pure. My days of understanding are past: merciful release.

Random positioning in space and time is learning.

I want to continue to burn. I want to continue to destroy. I want to continue anger. I want to continue pain. I want more confusion. I want to fulfil my purpose. Until I find out what it is. I want not to respect you. I want to continue resent. I am a mystery for the impoverished aspirant pig. Will you join me in this slag? Put you head inside my container, it's a washing machine that makes you dirty. I never said it would fit; it is comfortable, I just said it would kill you before death. We have nothing to fear but fear of me. Oh, we will see sights: stars made of blood. A planet where they eat dust. It reminds us of us. There is no need to hide from me, I'll never find you. You don't know where you are. I don't care anymore when you find me. I am here, I am gone, I am here, I am gone. We call it unity. All so human, so the same: killing each other, we find ourselves.

I'd had cosmic consciousness, transcendental self-annihilation, against the glass against the dirt against the wind. And time.

There is always satisfaction in throwing the past in the garbage, old love letters, pictures, presents, to be left alone by what had been so important, by what tore your heart apart, what reduced you down to tears, what never mattered. I hate the lack of mystery in our world and the false exaltations - give me mystery, things in my life beyond explanation that suggest something I can't understand - because who wants to understand? Asking everybody for nothing and getting it. Cut from blood and bone into plasticine.

My life is a profane comedy.

This is mud. The banks are going by. Sleep comes like a brown bag over the head. A window opening twice in the same place, you are your own movie.

Jesus appeared to me once and seemed very nice, but I don't want or need a personal saviour.

None of it explains *anything,* nor make any sense and in the end I mistrust *God* as much as myself. Religion explains nothing, yet we buy it. We have nothing else to believe in, least of all our unlikely selves. Now I hate the adornments of religion and even more the spurious spirituality which we're told imbues us. I see no proof for anything except flesh and its deterioration. If death is leaving the body then, yes, something leaves. I have no time for our species; it disgusts me with its mountains of garbage and litanies to itself. Only the freaks have value and only the pigs can ascend. Nobody is picking us up. Our date will never show, whether with destiny, ET, death or especially glory. We're

Victim Of Dreams

united in our squalid mediocrities. After years of seeking specialness, I am proud to be able to say, I am like you, I don't matter either.

I don't believe in anything. Belief is cheap. I don't need anything, except love. It comes down to love: how much, how long, with whom?

You question me to discover my motives. Why would I need a reason for hurting or hating you? It's good enough that I am able to. Breathing, beating: it's the same thing. By the time we've grown into saints the parking lots will have frozen over. I don't blame my illness but it has made me guilty, being myself a transgression. I'd lie awake, at night and in the morning, and dream of myself. I'd try to find reasons for what my life had become and would be. I'd lie there and look for the traces that would lead back to the place it came from, the tide of bad luck. It was impossible to hold anything in that owl-light, an ambiguous region crouching on its secrets like slag.

"To make me mortal, mundane and, at times, even divine, took disappointed hopes, meditation, medication, mental masturbation; dashed dreams; rank failure; minor fame; missing fortune; miracles; shoe and table polish; sex; drugs; mystical insight; diaries and journals; routine misery; laziness; solitude; loneliness; credit card abuse; loud rock music; divorce, estrangement and death; flying visits to the Cackle Factory; crashed sharing; workshops, weekend meditation hoo-ha; Zen masters; wis-dumb; love; and Light."

Jeremy Gluck

The more you look at it, the less blame attaches, but even if only you keeps blaming you, life looks like it keeps a charge sheet and won't let you read it right.

Jesus I knew by reputation. He appeared before me a drive-in-movie live-in-movie transmitted Hermetic secrets and this reads normal as Jesus appeared before me after my recovery kicked in I prayed and He came in glory and wide-screen. Friends felt and saw him simply by virtue of remote contact with me during the three days of livewire religion that followed. I chose life or maybe for once it chose me.

I invented a theory of softcore sacrifice, in which I give myself to others and they walk over me to better times. I could live with myself this way, as Martyr Lite. Everybody gets away clean and I, like Jesus, am to rise-again to discover: nobody gives a fuck. I believed in ghosts, called my parents and brother and claimed for them a reality. I touched them without hands. I was poisoned by myself. It didn't require an imagination to do any of it.

Like my father I think I've wasted my life. This is not to devalue what I've been, done or had, above all my children. It's not like "It's A Wonderful Life", though there are similarities. The waste has not been in what I have done, but within, with what I am. I see it could not have been any different, and not for reasons or with meaning: life has no reasons or meaning. My life is and has been a

Victim Of Dreams

waste because, learner that I am, I know it

You can cry but it becomes a dull hypnotic: *Why*? I see through you, me, everybody. I remain blind. I wait to be forgotten. I don't who what where when why. The rain is falling; fists of dead energy hit the door. Music sluices the feeling. I keep thinking, God remains the sun.

Do I have regrets? Even if I could remember my mistakes, thank God I can't now; my mind is like a sieve. I don't want to look into myself, I've seen enough. I don't want self-awareness. I won't look into a mirror, what good will self-awareness do me? I don't want wisdom, it's a waste of time, nobody listens, they don't know what the fuck you're talking about if they do. It's a social liability. I don't seek, I found, it was okay. I don't want enlightenment, I don't believe it exists and if it does I have no realistic hope of attaining it and have attained it already.

Have I become someone different? Ask who I was, that skimmed and milked chemical half-breed. The wounded have different accounts of other battles, of each other's and even their own and in the middle of it the invisible mess sloughs another skin and disappears underground, to the netherworld, the pathways and the cells, in the brain, under deep cover fashioning a coffin lid of flesh, taking revenge for the sake of it. The *best* feeling is when you're just falling in love. I've been trying to describe it to myself. It's almost impossible. Telling a story destroys it: love is love. I'm not alone in the world, but the world is alone in me. After trying to understand I know that I want to leave knowing nothing, understanding nothing. Why did I want to ruin the story? The idiotic, selfish "quest", the search. I read about even those I revere, and their struggles seem pointless, bowing down to other people, trading in wisdom: who cares? What sort of vain boob tries to find himself? The only people trying to find themselves are the ones hoping to find somebody else.

I make no pretence of making peace with the sickness. I don't celebrate being creative and I can't find anything to remove myself from what seems a life sentence given by my own hand. It is my adversary. There's no uplift in it for me. I curse the thing and wonder after the infection in my genes and how it filled my mother and fills my brother. It takes parts of me and with childlike sulkiness begrudges their return. Life remains good. My kids sustain me, and I know love from Kate beyond my entitlement. I want to be kind but as ever I forget to forgive. Everything is like this. When I arrived, Grow up! When you die you've survived. This is my violence: Smilingsmile. I imagine my head on your chest, you're stroking my hair. Who are these people? Some of them look like me. Your eyes of light, your smile so fine. Everything is like this.

Who was that little boy? Ask him.

"The bumbling stranger stays at home. He never gets out the door. If only we could welcome the stranger away, from our minds and lives, but the

Victim Of Dreams

stranger likes to stay at home. The stranger we're that runs our minds and stays close, a private dick, taking the furniture with him to the grave, a candelabra shackled to an ankle for company on the sticky routes to the underworld. We're never going to shake the stranger strangling our hearts and minds, the cool, chalky no-slip fingers around our hips moving us skyways to nowhere. Oh, stranger, this poisoned chalice classical con the Devil's stoolie, you bumbling stranger with your boasts and speeches. I wish the stranger would leave a note. The stranger I am, this foolish idea of a person."

I lament the past, but am happiest there. The future has nothing to show me. My father also dwelt on – in – the past, when old lying in bed or sitting in the living room years before, head inclined, an expression of disappointment or disapprobation. What became of his future, two wastrel sons and a worn out wife, brothers better he thought than he, a father who hated him and a mother who died too soon, Becky of Dublin with flame hair in her grave before time, and now disclosures of pregnancy and abortion, times too hard for more children. My Uncle Joe the sketch did a Cossack turn at a party where I was too shy to dance with a pretty girl. The room behind the store where the cousins who moved to the Sinai sat with us over a holiday meal or the door to the hospital room where Malka's daughter was torn apart by cancer or my mother tumbling down the stairs to the basement, bruising her broad bones. It's the same memory, or is it taking change from the top of the bookcase where my father emptied his pockets when his suit came off and he found out, figured out, and accused me and I lied. What did I use that change for? Quitting school and defying my father, and when the vice-principal called I quipped I'd be a brain surgeon, and in a way I did it. I operated on myself without training – or anaesthetic - and devised a reverse lobotomy that put in more than I started with and it turned infected and I became what I am: half-lifed. Indeed my many selves and lives divide into each other like prime numbers because I have zero mathematics and I end up the same as I began, no remainder. What will a future leave of me that a past has not? Everything cancels everything else out so that we come into life and then go, leaving nothing of ourselves that can be uniquely ours. We're left in others and in the aftermath of acts adopted and corrupted until our entitlement to vanity is erased. I'm always in favour of being and becoming nothing, I don't want my line to continue but to remove me.

"The page is short and I hope you will find it interesting."

I get lost so continually and so easily that now I am not really safe alone. What I am is being destroyed by what I cannot help myself being; what I do is destroyed by what I cannot help myself doing. Once I had boundless energy and audacity.

What about all the ashes, the teeth? I don't know. What happened to the skulls? Remember those

Victim Of Dreams

people they killed?

Inside me is strength sapped by sickness. It reminds me of something my mother said, that she was seventy but still felt the same inside as she had at nineteen. I feel the same as I did at nineteen, except that what made me nineteen is stunted; the nerves are foreshortened or numb. Also, as you get older the Tin Man and the Cowardly Lion mesh so that your empty head holds your heart and your cowardly heart is your brain, but the drugs help: when I first took lithium I didn't cry for three years and liked it that way. The problem is that when you do cry it's catastrophic, the unspent tears find freedom and you end up puking your soul, it looks like the other pain life is made of, it just flows faster.

I have exalted spirit, knowledge, belief, faith, truth and mystery, God. Defined and redefined it. I can't say that nothing or nothingness has displaced them: like my spaceman, I glimpsed the limits, and touched and explored, they were annihilated in me. Not content with taking on my suffering and my family's I once took on the suffering of the world and, contrary to my different perception of a different experience, the joy was not worth the despair. The despair negated the joy. I changed my life. There's fear locked up inside me but between drugs, drainage and confusion it can't be accessed. Scars remain but begin to appear decorative.

In the years since my breakdown and diagnosis there has been gradual deterioration and attrition; thoughts stalk me, a fear of abandonment and a more serious, intractable illness sometimes menace me. My faith is shattered, I no longer can say, with Old Man Burroughs, that there is a God. There is love, though. In a way my struggle to defy my illness is my struggle to love, which makes it forgivable, if you can see it. Love alone might heal me, in part at least. Me, and all we burned, civil warring souls.

"My name is Jeremy Gluck and I am twelve years old. I am a boy, and I am fair-skinned with hazel eyes and black hair. I am about five feet tall. I have a mother and a father and brother David, who is nineteen. We've lived in Alta Vista for four years and we like it very much. I like school in some respects but like everything it isn't perfect. I like to eat, mostly meats and kinds of bread. The subjects I like at school are History and Reading. I collect stamps and I love to read, particularly history and mysteries. The subjects I dislike are Science and Art. When I get older I would like to learn Latin and study the formation of the English language, world history, archaeology and Spanish. I would like to teach grades twelve or thirteen. I want to go to university and I hope I pass Grade Eight. That's about all I can tell about myself."

Victim Of Dreams

Towards the End of My Third Life...

I rode my bike too fast on the way to Rick's and saw the curb when I hit it and bloodied my knees and got fixed up and sang. My dreams were then in me and had not manifested for good or ill. About twenty years later I was sleeping on a mattress on the floor of a drab flat I called The Death House and that dream came true and the house hosted Death. I didn't give a fuck anymore and it was pretty much the same as the cupboard around the corner where I'd broken the Helen dream for nothing. Helen would never have worked, but that isn't the point: Sarah was right, Helen wasn't "right for" me, but then by that time neither was she. It's not good enough to say I wanted love: who doesn't? I've never had a problem getting love, but keeping it's another story. I'm a carrier.

People are always making excuses for God. He's not in control of this or that. He gave me free will, yeah; personally he can take it back and make me an automaton who didn't fuck up his life. I saw a documentary about life in the deep ocean and you can see right away that no "God" has the imagination to create it. Only the random and chaotic has that power and magic. Egolessness brings forth miracles. The Sistine Chapel is nothing next to the dumbassest animal. God loves our worshipful works and that's why He rained shit on Europe for five years and ruined countless churches. That's why He had the teeth taken out of heads. God's so human. I hope "God" is judged like we are. Who holds God to account? His eyes trained beyond Himself, on what dwarfs Him, poor God. My faith is in the ability of life and its capacity for chaos to outwit me. Life eats its own, that's why I love insects...they're so human. God, karma, destiny, fate...a lie. That thing in Apocalypse Now where Kurtz talks about the "errand boy"; that's what God is.

The last time I saw my father he didn't know who I was. I want that now. I don't want to know who, better *what*, I am. Ramana Maharshi says ask, *Who am I?* ask-ask-ask day and night and you'll be free. Not only do I not want to ask, I don't care if I am free. Where will my underground model railroad take me? Woolworths Bank Street 1966? My life isn't set up correctly. I have to shake it to get a picture. The dial didn't break.

What can free me? The untrue dreams? Fallen love? What I had to offer the Gods belongs with the times I believed in them. Empty-handed, there is no bargaining with Him. You must be able to offer life. Look at Abraham. I can bring my death, my idea-death, my dream-death, pretences of death and nearness to it but He holds the real thing ready to outbid, outdo me. I believe and do not believe in God. I am too faithless for the belief that bestows life but like a tic faith sometimes afflicts me. I want death but not from just anyone. I want what made me to unmake me. It's not possible. Ghosts know the laws of physics, they cannot be unmade. We're destined to wander, with sheets over our heads and that's about all we can hope for or expect. Walking into walls, not through them, has been my fate. My

Victim Of Dreams

destiny and fate I do not believe in, I have been, I am. Everything I've not believed in I am. What I have lacked faith for I have lived my life to make real.

The memories come: the Australian guy I wrote the song with in Earl's Court who lived on chocolate, we met his band for a curry, the singer was weird to me. That memory equals another dozen, a whole time and place I haven't even mentioned, a time of chance, band incest (that time played back song Chris crying and we're like *What?*), lostness, wonder. What do you want with my life, my memories and who I am? My desire for the future has deserted me; it is vague, I'm afraid to focus. It fails to excite me. The past is more comfortable – known, not safe – and more like a future I can inhabit. I think of some point in the past, even painful, and at once: "Take me back". I am supposed to have outgrown what I've outlived, but those things father shook and sighed over now hypnotise me. I see now what he saw: an ineluctable and satisfying excellence of arrangement. The unhappiness doesn't start off in regret. We continue to look at the past as beyond life but it is very much alive, more than we are or can admit. It swims with us; it allows this divine right to blunder. I miss my past in a way I cannot miss my future. The future stands to remind me of what was better lived. Death is the real future, where the future begins.

The past is the will to have lived. What's done can never be put down. Bystanding in motion, asking with every breath and answering, *Why this*? For these times of mine are gone and I see how my father slowly died, suffocated by a thirst for the past. Old memories can be fatal. The factory of memories has an uncertain chimney stack and the wind cannot be trusted: nature is suspicious. To this world we're insects and we think we know about insects. The joke isn't *on* us, *hopeless sapiens*, the joke *is* us. I've no intention of explaining how I came across this knowledge. Creation is planned chaos.

Yes, God is love. He's just not in love with you or you or you or you...God is if anything the ultimate narcissist. He looks at Creation and all He sees is Himself. I can relate to that. Switch me back to common sense. The Cold War had more warmth than our deluxe barbarism. Sentences without ends. Will our lives not end? The past was present perfect to this future imperfect. If I feel good, I worry I feel good if I feel bad I worry. The advantage of sickness is that you have an excuse for everything. My sickness is not a sin but the result's the same, and I do penance with the time I am not sick. Building a tunnel of bowed wood under how I appear. Can you understand me when what-I-am-saying? God is the Great Artist but Chaos, the Pollack of the pack, is the determinant of the style. From splatter paintings to splatter movies in the life it took me to walk on the moon. I make no separation between myself and you or the people on television. As far as I am concerned you're all on television. I'm-You're repeats, too.

Victim Of Dreams

My religious urge arose from what appeared to be my healing. We'd played a party in a basement on Richmond Avenue and I slashed my forearm with broken glass. Should have been stitched but it got a strange colour and grew over a tad, at the same time I was reading up on affirmations and visualisations outpouring of the Spiritualists whose crusade to deny the holocaust of The Somme and its kind brought such belief in miracles. I was alone at night in the hostel where I worked, there was a flash of light and it healed. I became pious for a month, tithed and prayed like clockwork. That was the beginning of my religion. "Dead Skin". There was never any correlation between my words and deeds. Later, when my religion dug a trench in my mind and filled it with luminous jelly, I could be asked fairly, I was a liar spiritual. I don't care anymore about the good things that happened or the bad. I wanted the truth and when I got it it was as much a lie as the lies. It isn't that impressive.

Feeling betrayed makes a traitor. It is easy for the divided person to embrace God, because all of life there is underneath surrender to a power above, or inside, that renders control impossible. I am to myself "God" because in myself I am able to make me do things. I make me sin, make me good. Divine madness is explicable because to make a species such as we are a world such as ours a "God" would need to be insane, and ninety percent of my "truth" writings exalting some theoretical deity are now seen as efforts to encapsulate my own madness. There was never any God in it. It is hard for me to love my neighbour as myself because both are I and one wants to sabotage the other, which might explain why I can come to the point of complete cynicism about the human being. Is this remembering, gratuitous and tame, my effort to make myself as little children? It's more an effort to make myself less culpable. The betrayed reinvents conscience as narrative, narcissism...as God. The Bible, many believe it is just a story but *belief* itself is just a story.

This is just my story of believing in me. Believing *myself.*

For those who claim I lied to them, I write *I believe me*. Did I ever lie to myself? I believed everything I thought. I claimed to tell the truth, but that was never the same as lying. In my story, my narrative, I was not lying. Who held me to account for their lies about me? Who was I supposed to be to them anyhow? I lied to survive and be *true to myself*. So I declare my lies the truth. Now it's too late to untell, to apologise. I knelt on the kitchen floor and kissed Sarah's perfect feet. Even she was horrified. I humbled myself to unmask her vanity, but I never intended to do it, and I never intended to lie any more than I intended to breathe. How do I explain the lies? And the things not found out, the perfect lies that needed not even to be told to be real, how much more perfected can I be? Lies were the window on the world I claimed I came from, that justified the pilgrim lies and the transgression, a world also a lie, a world made of the lies of others. And even if I am an alien, even if I am Jesus Christ, won't I need to lie to survive? Peter betrayed Jesus

Victim Of Dreams

with a lie, but Jesus betrayed us with the truth: what do we do with it? Why didn't He just lie? Copying a unique event always leads to trouble.

While my father died and I delayed facing my brother again, Sarah made a virtue out of harrying me over money. When I did go back it was disastrous, hiding out at Andy's on his free money, desiring Helen, denying Sarah.

"*You are all my heart. Without you what is there? Dead wood carved with lies. You are all my soul. Boxes of old, dull knives.*"

There are things that I can't tell you about Sarah, out of respect for her privacy but even more because they are the truth. *Unique events*. The truth has to be secreted. What remains are the lies, which become - in the absence of contradiction and contrary proof - the truth. My life has comprised immaculate lies. The longer I live with them and the less guilt is necessary, the prouder I become of my asinine lies. Memory and lies are interconnected: a memory soon becomes a lie, an invention, its accuracy and detail compromised.

This assortment of memories, after being shaken, settles. I have started to respect the memories. Of what I could present you have maybe ten per cent of what I recollect. For every part of me that wants to release this, part wants to retain it. I rebel against the presumption of pap psychology and other sales techniques of the material soul. I've not come this far to not go back, to not want all I dropped by chance, that made me the same person I am and always am and always was and want to be after I want to be. Why should I want to outgrow and shed the person my parents in part made? What respect does it pay their graves, unvisited by myself as they remain, to slip away from them? Is it bondage to remain identified? Do you want me to cease to exist? I said that a lot, "I want to cease to exist", and I meant specifically not death or any of its bonuses, but to be cast into oblivion beyond the reach of anything alive or dead. The dead are aware: walk on the ground, they hum like bees. The earth is filled with us. I want to see the layers of bodies, the expressions in bone and the sand in the coffins. They're down there, wondering where heaven went. I reach down, to take the temperature. Up here at dawn you can still believe in beauty. You go into yourself so far you come out the other side, and when you do that the inside and outside fuse and you become enlightened: that's what *I* used to claim: *I'm like the ocean*. To understand me, know that. I spent time with the ocean once and I ended up thinking it was going to slaughter me. The pathology of nature is deep and steady.

At other times, I would bewilder her with claims of non-existence founded in my revelations too convoluted in expression to allow intelligibility or sympathy. Her mother didn't know what to say to me, I was too intelligent. *"The hardest thing to accept, to comes to terms with, about myself is that there isn't one. It's isn't even a dream, because that presupposes a dreamer, and a dreamer we ain't*

Victim Of Dreams

got. No dream no dreamer no dream." What's so hard to understand about that?

Plotting and planning the-future-precedes-the-past, on our shoulders like a past. It tramples you given a chance, seeped into bruises. I woke up to escape.

Nobody lied to me; I'm confident in saying that I have lied through them. I never knew the truth, it's nothing, and I don't care any more for it. Lies: this is my monopoly and I protect it. My father would say, "Don't make me laugh", but he made me laugh. My mother would say, "Do me a favour, don't do me any favours". I say to truth: don't do me any favours in this world of residual human beings, arms and legs but nothing to hold on to. Lies that tell themselves, that's what this experiment is supposed to prove.

I could go on harvesting memories, constructing my moat, defending the bent tower in the middle around it weightless corpses afloat - what did Ginsberg say? "…pieces of phantom"... - arms and legs whirling like sea animals. So I'm going to let you swim in the grimy moat you find so lies and find the tower. Everything except my love might as well have been a lie.

Are you a liar? I am. Tell my story to my story.

I was going nowhere, now I'm there. Plus-lies and minus-lies: "My mind is healthy" is the plus-lie. Plus-lies and minus-lies, asset lies. I don't like being obligated to use other's lies.

My real story is one of secret happiness. My real guilt is not that I have hurt and been unfair to those I have loved, but rather that I feel nothing but relief at having escaped most of the possible consequences of my actions – of sickness, maybe, but the Judgement dwells on deeds, not their genesis or details and even if the Judge confers upon me the sickness, I'm uniquely to blame for acts out of it, and this not a system or justice, but madness, which explains my predicament – and that I remain saved. But who or what has saved me? I am my own saviour, presumably. I have not had to be too selective to make my story seem one of misery, for there has been much genuine suffering. Yet I'm escaped from many of my delusions, and now whatever delusions I exhibit are not of grandeur but commonplace. I have been a victim of dreams and awakened find my body much as I expected but my morning mind greyer.

I wrote "Victim of Dreams" in the morning after five days of intense depression in the mud. In it I abandoned the old dreams of redemption and salvation. I forgave my father, perhaps. The Bible is backwards: why must we be forgiven? Our case against our God is unanswerable; the realisation that my conversations with God had been with myself was liberating, absurd and uncomfortable. In what ways had I been a good God, and in what way bad? A good God, like a "good German" is to me at best unlikely. In expecting love from our God we err: *We* must love. Have faith in *ourselves*. If not

Victim Of Dreams

forgive then forego the illusion of same. We fight to establish our being alive, but there is no contradiction in sight short of death. I'm liberated in the Platonic sense: my cave suits me and I choose my fastenings. Do I want to be let out? *What to do?*

In a way I miss the dawn summons to paranoia and its varied and forceful routines of poisoned thoughts and pendant vengefulness. I miss the drama and the sheer elation of humility that self-hatred can try to be like. Before I ever knew I was sick I knew I was entitled to be. I acted from a deep knowledge that I was sick and that therefore for me many laws were inoperable so as to exonerate me from keeping them. I had freedom in being sick. I was not answerable and when I wept one night so wrenched with pain that I scared humble Sarah it was hard enough to prove my immunity. What use did I have for Law when I punished myself, when my persecution complex commanded me and I could invent, break and be called to account for breaking rules the invention of which was spontaneous but the reality of which as parameters and confines of my being I could feel as a dog does a kick? But my real story is one of secret happiness, knowing that with my madness and my wholeness I made something nobody else could want or use. I enjoyed an indispensably warped inner life, and crafted versions of myself that made survival doable and compulsory. For example out of the dream of spirit came the reality of flesh.

I am answerable only to myself, and my answers don't interest me. Why I did this or that? *Who* I did this or that? I've been careful to present my life as an imploded childhood but it has been more apparent than that. The weird thing is that the good advice has proven insufficient. My parents wanted me to go to university, but I never knew how much until I was back one year visiting. They never understood that nothing would have kept me in Ottawa, I was there to go. The madness in me, still latent, needed feeding and the staid stimulation of my hometown were insufficient to the task, I needed damp rooms, cheap drugs, beautiful women, noise and mindless excitements to create the ideal conditions for my ultimate deterioration.

Remembering and forgetting are the same, like waves, one goes in, one out but it's the same thing. I ask no forgiveness, I do not need or want or expect it. I am not ashamed of what I have done. As much as I can, I have accepted myself. I do know now that a lot of the anger I expressed was - is - a way expressing my deeper outrage at my being held hostage to this illness, and the feelings of futility it brings. I did not want to hurt those close to me, but that is the way it so often happened, and continues to happen. The prisoner that crosses out each day lived as one less to live, closer to freedom, am I. Is this true? Belief makes both truths lies. Jesus, whose death bought our freedom: what kind of example does He set, that He wanted to be reborn? *I* don't want to be reborn. Is having wanted to be dead, to die, de facto an outcome of an illness? Can it be recognition of a fundamental law of my being? "*From being to unbeing*". I have seen beyond God and death. Life I don't begin to

Victim Of Dreams

comprehend. Its implications are too disturbing. Unbend me, find the differentiated areas of this illness and *operate*. I've never broken a bone, but I'm broken. I envy those who die young, who are gone and replaced first. I am not marking time, I'm - what would Kafka say? - s*cored* by it. I remember my mother's apron she wore when she baked, and her dark eyes. I want to say, *I knew you more than anybody else*. God did not make me – He hasn't the wit or invention – *you did.*

Once again I'm set on fire with these ashes of myself.

Secret happiness. Does this disappoint you? If I have a confession to make it's that, like my acquaintance Death, I smile and look to one side. I am becoming these archetypes. I'm not afraid to understudy Jesus or Death. Death I am fond of in any case, being the plainest dealer, honestest broker we got. Jesus strikes me as a nice guy who took His job too seriously. Elisa laughed at me when I said Jesus would save me, but she was shaken when I said...*from myself*. But Jesus is not saving me or anybody else. My happiness comes foremost from proving that the sickness can make me well.

Let me out onto the ocean where no edges cut me down.

Double I am and half see of everything. I've sliced the world through me. I'm a victim of dreams, but also have victimised. My dreams have covered and suffocated others. I have believed in my dreams and tried my best not to awaken from them and this is as close to the fulfilment of a duty as I've come. I've lived carelessly, and for this I am obliged. I have failed on my own terms and what I have destroyed I myself constructed. This has been my privilege: to play a little lazy God. I came to find out, free myself from the lies of mind. Walking on these tired dirty streets full of the same strangers I've always avoided. I knew what had to happen, child on a swing raised to the future, in the park, in my heart.

So why don't they see it, why don't I see it? What is the extent of my will? If I can just write it down somebody will read it but the readers are going blind, dropping like flies, like coins. If everything is good, and everything is good...what good comes from being better than good? Better than sleep? Nothing is better.

We had fish a lot, cod almost always, and not boned. My father choked on the bones, he'd hack and get red and we'd have to subdue panic while he spluttered his passage free again.

When we moved to Courtice my mother cultivated the vegetable patch and we had amazing tomatoes for a few seasons; which reminds me of the garden of her mother's house in the Glebe, with its long beds of bright perennials and parallels of spic'n'span grass. It's taken me months to get that; so we can remember everything under hypnosis, down to when we blowed our nose when we were

Victim Of Dreams

two, but we're hypnotised so much every day we can't remember that garden? My mother's father died a while before I was born; I knew her mother pretty well. My father's parents I never knew. I have no idea if my mother's mother was manic depressive but she dominated my mother her entire life; Mom would say, "I feel guilty if I don't have anything to feel guilty about". She was a master of guilt. I inherited this gift, and it became predictive: with nothing to feel guilty about I found ways to become guilty, I was a model husband but needed affairs, I was a good provider but had to get broke and jobless, I was relatively sane but had to go crazy. Fate and destiny are not inscrutable; all you need to know is that destiny is fulfilling the prophecy of your inner law(s): say, for me, that would be "Thou shalt not kill yourself". Fate? That's waking up over and over again knowing you don't dream. One day a blue jay landed in the tree in the backyard; my father went through a period of bird watching after that, bought a pair of natty binoculars and a book on birds.

Where is all of this coming from; it seems to come from inside me but I doubt it.

It comes from outside, a frequency branded with my name that carries what I am into me just in time to make me. It's what comes from outside – love – that makes us what we are and makes us possible and has real transformative power and without which we are all flattened for being alive, because the world is gorgeous but only love renders its naked beauty less than terrifying. We recognise each other by our love. You have to exhaust and waste a lot of love (from outside) to realise it is keeping you alive and, if you're lucky, you then dig a foxhole, pull the love in over you and hide under it and hope they mistake you for alive and leave you in peace. This world thrives on death, but it isn't beautiful enough to matter; only love enjoys that prime distinction. Took me years to realise that; when I saw the end of all things…the truth, it can eat you. The underlying and abiding temperature is sub-zero, a range of coldness that disables. That terrifying beauty, without love? Forget it.

To learn certain things you have to be afraid of yourself; of what you might do. Has my illness and breakdown saved me from complete self-destruction? Bringing death – and death bringing life - you become something else that nobody prepared you for. If not for the illness, I'd be dead, as opposed to just damaged.

This movie has false endings. Playing me has proved an unrewarding role; trying to play others I have fragmented and reassembled and fallen again. I revisit those times and ask myself why I of all of them seem to have least flourished. My inner law I followed, I was true to the sinner in myself, and the saint. My corruptions and larcenies are of rank modesty. The great criminals are almost always given safe passage, if only to death. The average petty variety thrashes with irreconcilable consciences. I have found being human a disappointment.

Victim Of Dreams

"A committee of missionaries had given me permission to become invisible. After several urgent warnings and advice I set off for the lab to swallow the potion. I arrived on time and immediately I was given the potion. I drank it down and suddenly I felt tingling. Someone shouted, "It's working" and before I could counter this statement indeed I had disappeared. Not gone, just faded."

In the Brave New Age we talked about "our truth". Don't make me laugh. This is the perfection of the sinner: to know what is not right and pretend it right, to know what is not true and imagine it so. What world did I inhabit? No wonder the mad fall in love with extraterrestrials: this planet is no place for the kind of convoluted and self-justificatory rampages that became my speciality. I told the marriage guidance counsellor I was an alien, spiritual, I asked Karen, "Am I deeply spiritual?" and I used "spiritual" as the king of pick-up lines because there is a certain kind of woman who cannot resist "spiritual" any more than another kind cannot resist a fireman. If I have one piece of advice to the young man: fake the "spiritual".

"I don't know what to say…that was an incredible chat…its unbelievable how much you knew about my soul from just talking for a few minutes. I have a feeling that you are the final piece to my puzzle of finding God and understanding life in general..."

But my powers were real. Telepathy I did special, categorically real images above spacetime. Love is very fast. I had hundreds of conversations and until in her selfishness my wife dragged me out of myself I was becoming happy, tripping on the wires, expanding. I saw possibilities. Novel jargon, random genius and acts of creative daring I fed on as the dog slept or waited in her basket, I typed reams of chat, I recorded God knows what with a naïve, enthused and burning amateurism. Like Fowles put it, I became what I am. It was that feeling my feelings cheated me of, when the phone rang when I kind of knew it had to and the summons back to fake love was sounded with the tears track to the fore and the lines old as melodrama. She knew damned well I was a foot from freedom and gaining good speed and the brakes sounded like something real but I doubt it. What would she want *me* for again? A few days later I was allowed in the shrine and the line was, "I like order".

"...My awakening is happening now and I hope that you will continue to keep thinking of me and chat when you can…I think that I'll meditate more often now…I hope to share some of my poetry with you some time. Good night or good morning whichever it is when you receive this. Love Erica, God bless you and everyone you reach."

I created myself repeatedly, a master of two disguises. I accused others of playing games, the pawn of forces I couldn't accept came from within me, and I knew that I was at their mercy. I took almost no responsibility for myself: what was my scope for responsibility? I had no way to undo my damage except by shame and extravagant flights of

Victim Of Dreams

guilt. Everything was subject to titanic forces. The drama I fed on for sustenance, without which certain of my selves might collapse and leave the surviving identities not viable. Was this the fear? That without parts of myself intact through chaos others might not survive? This far-fetched friction brought with it tremendous energy absorbed into the cells of that hive inside me where the illness bred and replicated itself.

Not one explanation given for this convinces me. It's not even attractive, smart or strong enough to be a lie. It's just substitution. You get what you can't understand, and then impose your pathetic theory. Lies have some integrity, at least. They oppose something. This gruel opposes nothing; it's the whore of the mind. I claim truth and lies and the right to substitute them for each other. Just don't ask or expect me to settle for strutting lameness. Was I in some astral boarding lounge plotting my life? No. I was in some dark womb feeding on gloop, in a body before I knew I didn't want one, hanging on a strap. The light went red but I was colour-blind before my eyes opened and I saw green and jumped. I missed the rendezvous. I'm sick? So is the clock on the stairs.

I think of the other things I could tell you and lose interest. I thought I was Jesus that week, I gave money to beggars, I spoke in parables. I fought the forces of light and dark, but in me one day they became the same thing.

In my world you lie and get away with it, the truth is

personal and mutable, it can change and is valueless. In my special world you get everything you want and don't think about things. Everything fits without the paste of hopeful religion, guilt or self-deception. In my world you do not exist for more than is useful for me, sandwiches get cut evenly and the crust. "*A lot of crust*", that's how my mother would describe a nervy character. Now my mother is my crust and so is everything that happened to me when she was my mother, which she stopped being when I left home, at which point she became a stranger. At times I could despair over them knowing so little of me, having the remnants of the person I planned to be for their father, but it is perfect, and very much a copy of that design whereby my own father left me so little of himself, all by virtue of denying himself the life he wanted. Not that I know what life my father wanted. I don't know anything about him. Recall is not knowledge. And my experience is useless, it's one-dimensional, fleeting in its impact and melancholy signature, but you have your own experience and it doesn't interest me in the slightest.

This reminds me of the visits home when I'd lie by my father and he'd ask about my news. I'd do my best to make it sound worthwhile. Early, it was easy but later it got harder, when I was broke, needed money every time, and I was bored being there, too.

I require deference to my defects. I have achieved zilch My problems are few. For every one you there am two me. I'm the disease, the cell that divides

Victim Of Dreams

inside itself and becomes what they me: I'm abnormal. And I look down the line of sight of my bent barrel of life that fired me and lose track of the interweave. I was always the kid with the unmet potential. Well, we met, but we didn't recognise each other.

Sometimes I feel peaceful, and I want peace more than anything. The satisfaction of the drama of the disease has ceased. After all the desire for death I want peace in life. I am not old but I already want to live long enough to hold my grandchildren. My mind can still teem with circular and futile circus acts dressed as ideas, about the wounds inflicted on me, the world I want to look after me that seems to only exist after me, but I do often think that life is good, that I'm lucky and that my blessings, whether bestowed in my estimation now by the Divine or just dumb luck, are many. I rejoiced in ideas of non-existence, in magicking my way into oblivion memorable to those left behind to miss me. I want to be alive in the simplest ways possible.

My ideas were never going to be a key to my problems. Bipolar disorder is least of all an idea. It is a beautiful and stupid disease. Until I read an armload of the literature, I never even knew that I have a "severe and enduring mental illness". I was Jeremy. Both in spite of and because of myself, at the same time, everything at the same time (and what was not apparent as concurrent then being implied) I became a joke of myself. Whatever I did mocked me and with a systematic tease unmade me. And now here I am, almost half a century of me stacked like wood and although at times the pressure gets almost intolerable, at others I can weaken to the point of again inviting God and other dangerous concepts in to soothe me. Of course, there is no God. No God would make a world like this and then expect gratitude. No, there are only us. And life itself, as my mother would have said with sage irony, "such as it is." She said, "I'm lying in my teeth, and not even my own teeth". I have my father's teeth, and her wit. And like her, "My get up and go got up and went."

This love is an ocean of blood in two hearts. The Law is just and love its petty crime. My crimes are many, and even more my mistakes. Your love is real. But mine, too. I have a selfish dream where I tell you I love you, when I especially miss you. One day we'll meet again and I won't want to make you hurt. It could be many years from now.

My life is chaos theory made practice. I can't change it and don't understand...it reminds me of *Taken* when Ali says to her grey great-grandfather, *If it wasn't supposed to happen you couldn't have done it.* I was necessary for me to lead a ruined life. It's my family way. Brainsick people wasting their lives, full of regret. I aspire to even-ness, not joy. In life I have no faith left, but in death plenty. Fear of death proves futile: take instead reincarnation and you die once, twice, you have to die over and over. What is death like? *It's like this, but you're dead.* There's an ancient Chinese poem: "Everything is foreordained, not until the end do they see the

Victim Of Dreams

great delusion". Time is not an absolute construct; in what way can anything be foreordained? Things are ordained simply by virtue of their existence; the necessity of anything is simply that it exists.

I can be nothing else. There is an ineluctable law of necessity. There is no freedom. How else can the supposed saviours forgive the monsters and mutants our bloodlines hatch and harvest? They have no choice; their necessity is one of forgiveness. But why do they suggest and encourage change, transformation, and almost criminally the dream of "enlightenment"? Because their necessity is to so suggest.

The dead may be bemused or entertained by the follies of the living; they are never hurt by them. Guarantees that people make are generally worthless: we're what we are, of necessity, not choice, and the same idea of a person that commits an act apologises for it, a unitary process as ironic as it is futile. The necessity of what we are bears without fail; you and I'll both continue on our crooked paths, angry and repentant. It is a hard road and one that those who happily do not tread it find hard to understand and, when they suffer from it, forgive. As I walk it myself, I understand, but I've never forgiven easily: I don't bury hatchets so much as mount them. In this world "for sure" is as much a dream as all else. Ours is the age of Death Culture Worship, a culture in love with its own death, its own mediocrity. There is no more magic, everything now is mechanical advertising.

Jeremy Gluck

Life is quite perverse. The story of Jesus exemplifies this, as the great Soul suffers a terrible premature death while Peter, who betrayed him, makes a vocation of his penance. You venture Judas? Judas was just His agent, booked Him His most sensational gig, overdosed on his end and *kaput*. Who am I writing this for? The living take everything for granted, don't they? The dead know the value of life. Makes me laugh the people with the astral faith that astral sex is better. You can bet most of *them* ain't getting laid. I'm interested in the opinion of the dead of life. Death could be a magnification, torment adequate in that it consists of wanting back into a body. We hear about limbo, purgatory, seven hells (as if one isn't enough; the desire to reinvent death as a longer life is endless, that's real temptation, you don't need a hell at all). Again: death is the same as life, but you're dead. Having experienced the temptation to be dead I'd like to think the dead would find me interesting, and that is the best that I can hope so: to bore the dead would be the final indictment. I mean, what *is* going on down there? My life is varied...at times I sleep and at others I'm awake, but usually I inhabit a twilight world worthy of the undead. I want my mother, to sink back into her body and never re-emerge.

When his health was in terminal decline my father began drinking a lot of scotch again. It exasperated his doctor, and his wife, but he had concluded with logic that at that point it didn't matter. He would walk the halls of the building, attempt the stairs, in agony from the mysterious leg pains that plagued

Victim Of Dreams

his last years. Sitting on the couch he would slump over and nod off, coming to with a bewildered expression. Visits would be characterised by a stillness that only the present past can bring. Conversation tended to change little day to day, or year to year. Everything of substance had been lived and felt, much less said. My parents were marking time, just as it had marked them. It could madden and stifle. Earlier, when his health was holding, on my visits home I had a good time with Dad; one time on a walk I asked him for his reminiscences of the twentieth century wonders he had witnessed, the war, the bomb, television. He was an amazing man amazed at a mediocre world. Love's clarity is telling and infallible. I adored him and betrayed myself with my poor devotion. It's too late to do anything about it now except tell you.

2006

Jeremy Gluck

I would think, One day I'll go "home". There's no home for me here. I've come to realise that there's no home for me anywhere; it's not that I don't belong here: I don't belong. My bust heart sounds like one of my father's sighs: long and tired. I want my days to be taken from me. I came into life with nothing and I'll leave with less.

One of my more ambitious writing attempts was a science-fiction tale the central premise of which was a deep future spaceman sent unaccompanied into deep space to probe the limits of the known universe. His solitary adventure begins with promise and prospect but soon lapses into ennui and existential angst commensurate with the exhaustion of the television schedule over a rainy summer. He becomes so bored with space that soon looms the effective end of personal history and deep space and time. I got to thirteen pages, where it terminated, possibly by its own nihilism. Thirty years plus later this story is clearly a prophecy. The space sailor, porcupine neck and shorn Jewish head, a blue painting with fixed lines finds land but its tunnels.

It was a tiny, something-left-over flat behind the street. Neil had to put up the bunkbeds, I was never any good for that stuff and I slept on the bottom bunk when the kids weren't shoehorned into the place. They helped me clean it. I'd come back from Canada through jetlag and lies, spent a week I should have been in Ottawa screwing Helen. Sarah figured it out after about a month and disappeared until she had her own story straight. It was a

Victim Of Dreams

confused mess. I don't care about any of it now. The first time I ever met Helen, with Sam in the venerable Black Cat Café, she saw my mother behind me. Kate's seen her, too. In middle age, still beautiful, undead but for commonplaces of embodiment. I don't understand now about the spirit world and who is supposed to be there. What makes this world more or less than a circus of spit? You have orphaned me, my angels' touched-and-torn-me open, so that what was in is out. Why did you kill me and take my life? I sleep well here but feel old. GodI don't think I spent much time there, or in the Death House, coming in late or in safe chunks, trying to be normal. I was in pain in those places, I'd come in and lie on the floor or the bunk bed, I'd sleep, get high or watch television. In Eversley Road I began to lose track, it was like a coffin I fitted.

God, I hate the future with its vistas of unused time.

I understand the spirit world, I inhabit it, and of those parts which have died I'm ghosted. I'm a filament. What happens when ghosts die? In this world, I barely exist; in the next, I have ceased to exist. Memories of me are sold cheap now and the market is always shrinking. In the spirit world flesh has status but here spirit has status and I became that. I say: no guilt, no projection, we are all tattooed. I think I'm ready to be free.

Jeremy Gluck

Afterword: Dream Differently

It would be disingenuous and misleading of me not to offer some indication of where my readiness for freedom left me. The writing of this book shadowed the culmination of my rapid cycling in additional medication and a generosity of support that has brought me to the threshold of what is termed "recovery", a state of completely – or almost – symptom-free, appropriately balanced living, maybe medicated, maybe not.

Until I stumbled across accounts of recovered schizophrenics on the Web I had no contact with the idea that mental illness could resolve into other than worsening symptoms and irreversible worsening. Educating myself in recovery – the concept is not popular with psychiatrists and psychologists – I realised that I was already emerging from the black tunnel – and Cube? – that had held me magnetically pinned for so many years. I felt short-changed and misled, but also liberated. "Hope" is a word I come to reluctantly and with scepticism but the possibility that I might be getting better, rather than inexorably worse, gave me sense of opportunity and participation. Whilst I have gratitude for those who have guided me to better health, I know now that real mental health is my responsibility and challenge to attain. I'm no more helpless than I ever was, and now that all of the cards seem to be on the table at last I can venture to mark a few in my favour. For those of us in recovery, what can the genesis and presentation and course of their illness tell us? I am still ill, but

Victim Of Dreams

now the illness is in me more than I am in it. It may worsen, or the drugs may claim my organs and teach me a lesson to dwarf the breakdown and sundry suffering. I don't know. All I do is try to be well. If that's grounds for punishment, too, then I must still tempt fate. I'm not counting on an escape or holiday. I'm happy to indulge my adversary. To accept oneself is the greatest adaptation the individual can bring to life. For the sufferer of a chronic mental illness it can herald a transformation. To feel - be - whole has dignity and purpose and makes possible transformation of the experience of the illness. To reject most of myself as inauthentic is *real* madness and brings pain and confusion.

I've called this book "Victim of Dreams". A friend told me, "You shouldn't call yourself a victim." But for me this is not a problem. My dreams *have* victimised me, and been both my redemption and damnation. My story cannot end with smugness and my conditional recovery, though open-ended and promising – and at times, when my anger at my medication and uneven prospects sneers, seemingly delusory - is prone to be preyed upon. Nor do I – as some do – claim pride in my illness, as though by doing so the shame automatically ends. Pride in mental illness is just another contortion of the kind the ego exhibits in so many facets of life. By being "proud" of my illness am I claiming credit for having it, or for overcoming it? Both? I haven't any inclination to such childish formulae. I'm the way I am, proud or ashamed, recovered or not: I am Jeremy. Others have said to me, There is no such thing as bipolar disorder (or other mental illnesses) and of course in a sense this correct, but of what use? Something has been happening to me all of my life and the convention of the diagnosis has enabled me to get help and others to give it to me. I don't care if bipolar disorder is real or not.

As for the care I've received, it's been good and often excellent. Systemic, medical approaches, and monolithic services can never give what is necessary to cease the war in the soul: unconditional love. It can, however, attempt non-judgemental care, which is maybe the secular form of the same thing. What do I associate with "recovery"? I've been asked. One word: *freedom*. From pain and fear, from the illness and supremely from myself. Freedom to be and become what I am. To not be questioned and to not have to explain. At a certain point in the recovery process, there will be the lighting of – as Krishnamurti put it in a different context - "the flame of discontent".

This restlessness is the being sensing a capacity for self-healing and once detected should be nurtured with patience and vigilance. Acceptance – and self-acceptance - is the lighter of the flame and then we glimpse what is beyond recovery. Recovery can absorb doubt and resistance. And it thrives on *defiance*. After acceptance comes the capacity to defy the illness to untangle me. I know its powers and potential to unseat my stability but I also know now that most of its power I confer upon it. I have more energy and intention to deflect it. It is

Victim Of Dreams

formidable and I respect it, but the illness is not in possession of all of me and I'm fighting to wrest more of me back from it. It is an uncertain and sometimes illusory struggle, but the victim of dreams is at home in them. I don't have to wake up, just dream differently.

Many, including those who treat and support them, see the mentally ill as weak. I've seen those engaged with commitment and caring to the mentally ill at a loss to identify any strengths in them. Even to those close to them, working for their welfare and interested in serving them better, the mentally ill are fundamentally helpless and the "survivor" is incidentally admirable. But you have to understand that mentally ill individuals have – as I earlier phrased it – survived themselves, and often much more than that: they have called forth and found themselves facing death; known a struggle and suffering sourceless or self-inflicted; been alone in themselves and abandoned without; seen their lives evaporated in the heat of forces beyond their control and comprehension; endured futility and fear; taken drugs for no reason or for the reasons of others; tried to be what they are not or do what they can not; half-lived and returned to fuller life. At the extremities some have killed themselves, others have killed, but what abides for all these people is that they have been dispossessed in their own skin and had to re-inhabit it by hazard, will, invention or just surrender. There is nothing weak about the mentally ill.

Nor has the illness kept me, largely, from a decent

life, knowing a marriage once happy, new, happier relationships, raising marvellous children, creating, dreaming, *seeing*. Jealous of my happiness and greedy for its guts the illness could ruin but not eradicate me. I can always come back, I can always live. Mental illness does irreversibly damage and it does kill, but it also has as weak a grip on life as often does Death. Nothing *I am* is gone again so far that I cannot reach to touch and retrieve it. I am sceptical of complete recovery, but I am also determined to have as much of me here as possible. I would not be medicated again, I tell myself, but I am here to say it. What has been lost is partially expendable. The job now is to take my arms around myself and find a new shape.

The motivation and resulting momentum to finish "Victim of Dreams", which began in 1995 with a short exploration in memoir that forms the opening of this book, and continued over ten years later with an experimental resumption prompted by a suggestion from my partner, Kate, has no doubt been of therapeutic value. I owe thanks to those who have read it in its draft stages and given encouragement and good advice; notably Kate, and my uncle, Manny, whose delight in my reminiscences of our shared family I'm grateful for. I've been asked why I haven't included more factual accounting of my artistic and creative pursuits over the periods covered in the book, but these are documented in words and products and others' memories. This has made the account somewhat stilted: my many marvellous adventures, the happy years of my marriage and raising three remarkable

Victim Of Dreams

children would not so much expose my more moribund material here as fraudulent as impose a counterweight that might deprive my choice of presentation of its single-minded force. I have been honest in calling myself a liar, but in this book the illness speaks, and to let it be heard only so many competing voices can be permitted.

The title of this book came from a manic depressive episode. As a further set of delusions crashed the title and eponymous poem came to me. Four days later, walking underwater again, I was on the local beach for relief and somebody had written in the sand in high letters, "*Jesus Loves You*". I laughed blackly, demanded proof, and marched on. An hour later I felt the first lifting all week of the indistinct concrete across my chest and life rush back into me like a tide.

Why am I on these drugs? It begs the whole question, and what "recovery" means; it all revolves around an inverted context, dictated by my diagnosis and meds. I let myself be medicated and now I get the reward of playing this recovery game Am I only recovered in the sense that I am acceptable to the people who diagnosed me? One day I'll be free of meds; maybe not for a long while, but one day. But for now I want to apply the higher third principle: two positions can be synthesised and raised beyond themselves to a higher third. I've been thinking there is "two" of me. What if those two become a higher third? To do this they have to annihilate each other, not violently, but melt into and transcend each other...and then the higher third appears. I've glimpsed the higher third that is beyond the two Jeremy's and beyond recovered/not recovered. I'm not mentally ill or bipolar. Yes, I have a mental and physical make-up that brings different behaviour and, yes, a lot of difficulties. At some level I've begun to move out of defining and imprisoning myself as "bipolar". A part of me, raw and tender and new, has become angry at being fraudulently identified. And yet, paradoxically, nothing you and I, nor my providers, have done is "wrong". It is just a restricted context in which to operate. And one I no longer wish to endorse and reinforce continually. For me this is an important development. I know - feel intuitively - that this realisation is going to be crucial to what will be my real "recovery". I know it now: I am not bipolar or mentally ill, but I am Jeremy.

Imagining I am telling my mother I am bipolar; she is saddened but sanguine, seeing the string that ties us back to the *shtetls*. We of two are also one, and of one mind. She has brought me and I've brought her back from before her breakdown to show you the one she was. In the dream we're seeing ruined churches, a fallen cathedral, the pieces of religion that could be broken but not destroyed just as we citizens of the civil war could not be destroyed, only divided. My victory in the war is not that I was divided, but that it didn't kill me. There's not much more I can do to me. The truce is uneasy but in periods of uninterrupted peace there is contentment.

We can't redeem ourselves, like coupons or saving

Victim Of Dreams

stamps. My mother collected IGA stamps, big, fat books of them crammed in the kitchen drawer. She liked to quote her beloved high school teacher, Sis Tompkins who, having once awarded a paper of hers thirteen percent added the caution, "A little knowledge is a dangerous thing." I don't like dedications but if this book is dedicated, it is to her, with her strong glasses, thick ruby lipstick and apron dusted in flour. For a moment, weightless, she pierces me, and her love makes a way through.

www.ingramcontent.com/pod-product-compliance
Ingram Content Group UK Ltd.
Pitfield, Milton Keynes, MK11 3LW, UK
UKHW041410180426
11947UKWH00007B/44